Praise for S

Suzanne Gross provides an exquisitely written, painfully personal account which will enable readers to understand what life was like for a French Jewish child during the terrifying Nazi years 1933 - 1945. It is carefully documented with archival material, photographs and letters. This is a much needed addition to the historic and literary information about the Holocaust in France and the complicity of the Vichy government. I am grateful to Ms. Gross for providing this rich and readable volume for teachers to use in the classroom. *Sarah Dreams Of Pitchipoi: A Hidden Child's Memoir Of The Holocaust In France* will serve equally well to those who continue to struggle with the deeply disturbing question; how could one and a half million innocent children been sent to their death?

Dr. Marcia Sachs Littell
Professor, Holocaust and Genocide Studies
The Richard Stockton College of New Jersey

To read of Suzanne Gross' memoir of her childhood in Nazi occupied France is to begin to comprehend what life must have been like for Jewish children who were guilty of nothing more than being born as Jews...

Elaine Culbertson, Chair
Pennsylvania Holocaust Education Council

Sarah Dreams of Pitchipoi

A Hidden Child's Memoir of the Holocaust in France

by

Sarah Suzanne Gross

COMTEQ PUBLISHING
MARGATE, NEW JERSEY

Published by:
ComteQ Publishing
A division of ComteQ Communications, LLC
P.O. Box 3046
Margate, New Jersey 08402
609-487-9000 • Fax 609-822-4098
Email: publisher@ComteQcom.com
Website: www.ComteQpublishing.com

ISBN10 0-9793771-4-5
ISBN13 978-0-9793771-4-3
Library of Congress Control Number: 2007943551

Cover design by Jackie Caplan
Book design by Rob Huberman

Archival photographs and documents were researched by the author at the Centre de Documentation Juive Contemporaine (C.D.J.C.) in Paris, and at the Institute for Jewish Research (YIVO) in New York.

Printed in the United States of America
10 9 8 7 6 5 4 3 2 1

This Book is Dedicated to

1.5 million Jewish children who perished in the Holocaust

Aunt Perla Cogan deported to Auschwitz on September 25, 1942, in convoy #37 from France.

Uncle Avram Cogan deported to Auschwitz on September 25, 1942, in convoy #37 from France.

Cousin Volf Cogan deported to Auschwitz on September 25, 1942, in convoy #37 from France. Selected for slave labor and sent to the camp of Blechhammer/Auschwitz IV.

Cousin George Cogan, arrested and interned in the camp of Drancy.

My childhood friend Michel.

My childhood friend Marguerite.

Forever Grateful to

The two "Righteous Persons" who kept my family and me alive while in hiding:

Madame Blanchard

Chaouche

In Memory of

My father, Eli, who fought back and joined the Jewish Fighter Brigade.

My little mother, Chaike, with whom my sister Charlotte and I shared our hiding place.

Contents

Preface

I was once told that the drop of the stork makes all the difference in one's future because it determines everything that will happen in a life. If you are born on the right side of the tracks you will experience something quite different than someone who has the misfortune of being born on the opposite side. To read Suzanne Gross' memoir of her childhood in Nazi occupied France is to begin to comprehend what life must have been like for Jewish children who were guilty of nothing more than being born as Jews, a fateful drop of the stork in the time before and during the Second World War and the Holocaust.

With painstaking research, Suzanne has been able to document the chronology of events that turned her once happy childhood into a time of pain and loss. Through her words and skillful juxtaposition of photographs and documents (in the original and in translation for those who are not fluent in French and German) the reader feels the world constricting for French Jewry. We see the restrictions and expulsions, the attempts at hiding and, most poignantly, the loss of childhood. Suzanne establishes very clearly what was taken, a life filled with Yiddishkeit, a home where parents had dreams and aspirations for their children, a community where the children felt safe and accepted by their neighbors whether Jewish, Christian, or Muslim.

To read this memoir is to gain a sense of what it must have been like to watch your parents rendered helpless and wonder whether you would survive. Suzanne's memoir is personal, but she extends the story to include cousins and friends who suffered different fates. Through their experiences she is able to tell the full story of what happened to families and especially to children at the hands of the Nazis.

In France, the Nazis seem to have functioned less efficiently than our stereotype of their bureaucratic machine. The decision to deport Jewish adults left thousands of children alone, with no means to deal with their new situation. The resulting chaos drained the resources of the Jewish community and caused intense hardship for the very young. Though she herself escaped that fate, Suzanne documents the stories of friends who have never recovered physically or psychologically from their abandonment.

For the teachers who want to introduce their students to document analysis and photo interpretation, this book is a treasure. Suzanne's story is appealing and well-told; and for those who are still trying to understand what happened, and there are many of us, Suzanne's holocaust memoir is one more piece of a very complex and challenging puzzle. If Pitchipoi exists, we are no closer to it now than we were then.

Elaine Culbertson

Elaine Culbertson is the chair of the Pennsylvania Holocaust Education Council, a statewide organization of teachers, survivors, and liberators who volunteer to keep the lessons of the Holocaust alive in the schools of the state. Elaine represents the United States Holocaust Memorial Museum as a museum fellow and a regional educational consultant in the MidAtlantic states. She is the program director of the Teachers Summer Seminar on the Holocaust and Jewish Resistance, a program that has taken almost 800 teachers to Poland and Israel for advanced study of the Holocaust over the past 22 years. She works with teachers and students to connect the events of the past with the genocides of the present day. Elaine has written and lectured across the United States, using the story of her own parents' survival as the basis for her presentations on developmentally appropriate and morally responsible pedagogy. She first met Suzanne Gross when Suzanne visited the school where she served as principal in 1999.

Introduction

Of the six million Jews killed by the Nazis during the Holocaust, close to 80,000 of them were French and foreign Jews deported from France, and around 11,600 of those were children. There is much to be told about their young lives and the premature end of their existence. In fact, there are so many stories that can never be all told. What I have attempted to do is to interweave elements of three separate stories that, together, will enable you to understand something of what those times were like.

The first story is how, in order to save my life, my parents arranged for me to be hidden from the Nazis and the French police, on my own at the age of ten, both in Paris and in the French countryside during the dangerous time of the Holocaust. The second is the larger story of the Nazis' efforts with the active participation of the French Vichy government to identify, separate, deport, and ultimately murder the Jews of France. And third, is the story of how those efforts affected Jewish children in particular—both those like me who survived—and those who did not. In order to tell and authenticate these stories, I have included archival documents, which were researched at the Jewish Archives in Paris and New York. They show the close collaboration between Vichy France and the Nazis in the deportations—and photographs from my own family, as well as those from the collections of brothers and sisters who survived their deported siblings and parents.

Why have I told my story of the Holocaust and that of the children of Pitchipoi? I have done so because mankind almost lost its human soul while it happened...and because it must be told...because this threat must not be buried in silence and denial, also because the memory of innocent victims must not be abandoned. Hopefully, knowledge of this man-made cataclysm will prevent it from happening again.

Sarah Suzanne Gross
Philadelphia, 2005

CHAPTER ONE (FOREWORD)

Sarah Dreams of Pitchipoi

Pitchipoi: the ending "oi" is pronounced "oy" as in boy.

This memoir is titled *Sarah Dreams of Pitchipoi* because, for the first nine years of my life, I was Sarah. A never-never land called Pitchipoi was rumored by the Jewish children interned in the French concentration camp of Drancy to be the destination of deportation.

No one knew what and where Pitchipoi was, but since the people in the camp were told that they were going to "an unknown destination," as sometimes happens in desperate situations, the children found a way to hope; for those separated from their mothers and fathers, they perhaps might even be reunited in Pitchipoi.

Pitchipoi was actually a name that came from a Yiddish/Jewish folk song originating from Poland. Its oral transmission and transformation has been demonstrated in a fine analysis by historian and musicologist Leizer Ran, in Padres—1992 #16.

In 1939, there were 70,000 Jewish children in France, or about 21 percent of the total Jewish population of about 333,000. Of these, 11,402 children were deported. Are these innocent young lives remembered till this day? Yes, they are imprinted in our soul: Suzanne had a dream where Sarah, on one of her visits in heaven, met with the 11,402 children of Pitchipoi. They asked her if those who are still on earth knew the story of their treatment and deportation from France to Auschwitz. Sarah answered that "survivors" such as Suzanne are writing and speaking on their behalf so the world will be forewarned about anti-Semitism, racism, genocide, persecution, denial and indifference. She also told them that their innocence is forever remembered.

*****

I was born in Paris of Russian immigrant parents. My childhood was filled with the wonders of a rich Jewish cultural life, marked by a passion for learning, and I lived in an atmosphere of unconditional parental love. That was until the summer of 1940, when the Nazis invaded and conquered my beloved country. Not long afterward, because my biblical name was uniquely "Jewish" in France at the time, my parents decided that to protect me I should be called Suzanne instead. That would be the beginning of my hidden identity. To this day, I am called Suzanne. Yet, through all the years since the German invasion of France, Sarah has stayed hidden within me, as have Sarah's haunting memories.

As a "Hidden Child" during the Holocaust in France, I learned the importance of being silent, and even after the war for many years I did not speak of my experiences. Although I physically regained my freedom when France was liberated, my soul was not free to tell my story. It took a long time to confront the extent of the murderous destruction. I felt that since I had not perished anonymously, like my loving aunt and uncle in Auschwitz—or lived through the unimaginable horrors of camps such as Birkenau, Buchenwald, Chelmno, Mauthausen, Sachsenhausen, Belzec, Sobibor, Treblinka, Majdanek and many more—I had not suffered.

Now, however, at this time of my life, a language both spoken and unspoken has arisen from the ashes. And those like me—the last generation of children old enough to have experienced and to remember anti-Jewish persecutions first hand—can now tell for the sake of humanity the horrors that our eyes have seen, the cries our ears have heard, and the misery that was. As one of those whose existence and life was threatened by the most inhumane crimes that man ever perpetrated against man, woman, and child, I am compelled to bear witness for the children—some of whom were my family and childhood friends—who were unmercifully silenced forever.

Because there is much that is not commonly told about the 4051 children among the 11,402 Jewish youngsters between two and fifteen years old who were deported from France and because their victimization stands in stark contrast with the many reassuring tales of rescue, there is a need to tell their story. They were *The Children of Pitchipoi.*

Pitchipoi, for some, was a far-off destination of hope, while for others it was an unfamiliar voyage of despair. The Jews in the transit camp of Drancy had been cut off suddenly from their everyday lives and separated from their loved ones. None of them were told where they were being sent, other than to an "unknown destination." It was during the fatal days of July 16 and 17, 1942 that over 4,000 youngsters and teens had been caught in the very first immense round-ups of Jewish women and children in and around Paris. Individuals without children were interned in the transit camp of Drancy and families with children were kept in the camps of Pithiviers and Beaune-la-Rolande. They were to be moved to Drancy when their deportation took place.

Since men had been rounded up and deported first, at one point there were not enough of them arrested for deportation to the "East" to meet the minimum quota of 1000 souls required per train. So mothers were separated from their children to complete the scheduled transports. (According to a report filed with the French Committee of the Red Cross in London, when the mothers resisted, French police used truncheons to beat and control them and the children.) That left over 4000 children without their mothers and fathers. Although Gestapo Chief Dannecker had argued that the children should be deported with their parents, otherwise, "the children would come under the care of the French welfare system, and since extended contact between Jewish children and non-Jewish children was undesirable, it would be best to deport them immediately." (Archives of July 6 and 10, 1942).

But neither the children nor their elders were going to Pitchipoi. On July 31, 1942 mothers began to be loaded onto cattle cars, ahead of their children, to fill the quota of 1000 Jews per convoy. Only a month later, following the approval by *SS Hauptsturmfuhrer* Eichmann* and the acquiescence by French President Laval to deport the children, a planning meeting took place with Dannecker, Gestapo Chief of the anti-Jewish section in France. Also present at the meeting were the French Vichy police representatives who were in favor of the plans.

The children were deported without their parents at first, which produced a disastrous sight at departure at the train station. Mindful of appearances, in order to make it look like the children were being deported with their families, Berlin ordered by telex (see archival telex of Aug.13, 1942-secret-urgent, page 13) that "any convoy from Pithiviers and Beaune-la-Rolande to Auschwitz should not be made up exclusively of children."

*Adolph Eichmann: SS in charge of the German headquarters in Berlin for the implementation of the "Final Solution." He was appointed to department IV B4 of the Gestapo in Berlin, which handled ways to dispose of "unwanted" Jews. His department had created gassing techniques, death camps and systems of convoys to take European Jewry to their death. His previous civilian work experience in oil companies taught him how to organize timetables, deliveries, and to identify sites of communication junction. Eichmann systematically applied the logistics of commerce to the annihilation of Jews during the Holocaust.

R. F. SS
Sicherheits-Dienst
Nachrichten-Uebermittlung

Aufgenommen Tag Monat Jahr Zeit von durch	Befördert Tag Monat Jahr Zeit an durch	Raum für Eingangsstempel
Nr	6. JUL 1942 Verzögerungsvermerk	
Telegramm – Funkspruch – Fernschreiben – Fernspruch		

urgent! forward immediately!!
============================

Paris, July 6,1942

To the
Central Security Office of the Reich
- IV B4 -

B e r l i n

<u>Subject:</u> Deportation of Jews from France
<u>File:</u> Meeting between SS Obersturmbannfuhrer Eichmann and SS Hauptsturmfuhrer Dannecker on July 1, 1942, in Paris.

All the stateless Jews of the occupied zone and the unoccupied zone are ready to be turned over to us for evacuations.

President LAVAL has offered the Jews from the unoccupied zone, including children under sixteen years of age, to be taken along. The question of Jewish children left alone in the occupied zone is of no interest to him.

Therefore, I urgently request that you send an order by telex to start including children under sixteen years of age with the fifteenth convoy of Jews.

In closing, I would like to bring to your attention that until now we have not been able to even start any action regarding stateless Jews, in the second phase [of this operation], we will go after Jews naturalized in France between 1919 to 1927 respectively.

Signed: Dannecker - SS Hauptsturmfuhrer

Archival telex of July 6, 1942

R. F. SS
Sicherheits-Dienst
Nachrichten-Uebermittlung

Aufgenommen Tag Monat Jahr Zeit von durch	Befördert Tag Monat Jahr Zeit an durch 6. JUL. 1942	Raum für Eingangsstempel
Nr	Verzögerungsvermerk	

Telegramm — Funkspruch — Fernschreiben — Fernspruch

IV J SA 225a dringend ! sofort vorlegen !

Dan/Bir

Paris, den 6.7.1942

An das
Reichssicherheitshauptamt
- IV B 4 -
Berlin

Betr.: Judenabschub aus Frankreich.
Vorg.: Besprechung zwischen SS-Obersturmbannführer Eichmann und SS-Hauptsturmführer Dannecker am 1.7.1942 in Paris.

Die Verhandlungen mit der französischen Regierung haben inzwischen zu folgendem Ergebnis geführt :

Sämtliche staatenlose Juden der besetzten und unbesetzten Zone werden für den Abschub bereit gestellt.

Präsident LAVAL hat vorgeschlagen, beim Abschub jüdischer Familien aus dem unbesetzten Gebiet, auch die unter 16 Jahre alten Kinder mitzunehmen. Die Frage von im besetzten Gebiet zurückbleibenden Judenkindern interessiert ihn nicht.

Ich bitte deshalb um dringende FS Entscheidung darüber, ob, etwa beginnend mit dem 15. Judentransport aus Frankreich, auch Kinder unter 16 Jahren mit abgeschoben werden können.

Abschließend sei noch bemerkt, daß, um die Aktion überhaupt in Gang zu bringen, vorläufig nur von staatenlosen bezw. fremdstaatigen Juden gesprochen werden konnte. In der 2. Phase wird dann an die nach 1919 bezw. nach 1927 (in Frankreich) naturalisierten Juden herangegangen werden.

1)
2)
3)
4)
5) Z.d.

7/7/42

Urgent, forward immediately!

IV J SA 225 a

Paris, July 10,1942

NÜ 1326

Befördert durch N. Ü.

Tag Monat Uhrzeit

10 JUIL 1942

an App. durch

To the
Central Security Office of the Reich
- IV B4 -

B e r l i n

Subject: Deportation of Jews from France

File: Conversation between SS Obersturmbannfuhrer Eichmann and SS Hauptsturmfuhrer Dannecker on July 1, 1942, in Paris, my telex of July 6,1942, Dept. IV J SA 225 a.

The arrest of stateless Jews in Paris will be carried out by the French police beginning on July 16 and ending on July 18,1942. We may expect that approximately four thousand Jewish children will come under the care of the French public welfare system. Since extended contact between these children and non-Jewish children is undesirable, and since the U.G.I.F. can only accommodate a maximum of four hundred children in its own children's home, I am making an urgent request for a decision (via telex) concerning whether the children of these stateless deported Jews can also be included, along with the tenth transport.

I am simultaneously repeating my urgent request for a decision concerning the question raised in my telex of July 6, 1942.

I.A.

SS - Hauptsturmführer

XXVb - 58

FS.

Dringend, sofort vorlegen !

IV J SA 225 a   Paris, den 1o.7.1942
Rö/Bir

NÜ 13265

Befördert durch N. Ü.
Tag 10 JUIL 1942
an durch

An das
Reichssicherheitshauptamt,
IV B 4,

B e r l i n

Betr.: Judenabschub aus Frankreich.
Vorg.: Besprechung zwischen SS-Obersturmbannführer Eichmann und SS-Hauptsturmführer Dannecker am 1.7.1942 in Paris, mein FS vom 6.7.1942, IV J SA 225 a.

Die Verhaftung staatenloser Juden in Paris wird von der französischen Polizei in der Zeit vom 16.7. - 18.7.1942 vorgenommen werden. Es steht zu erwarten, daß nach der Verhaftung etwa 4000 Judenkinder zurückbleiben. Für diese Kinder soll zunächst die öffentliche französische Wohlfahrtspflege eintreten. Da ein längeres Zusammensein dieser Judenkinder mit nichtjüdischen Kindern unerwünscht ist und die "Union der Juden in Frankreich" in ihren eigenen Kinderheimen höchstens 4oo Kinder unterbringen kann, bitte ich um dringende FS-Entscheidung darüber, ob die Kinder der abzutransportierenden staatenlosen Juden etwa vom 1o. Transport ab mit abgeschoben werden können.

Gleichzeitig bitte ich nochmals um dringende Entscheidung über die in meinem FS vom 6.7.42 aufgeworfene Frage.

Vfg.
1) IV J 3
2)
3)
4)
5)

I.A. Dannecker
SS - Hauptsturmführer

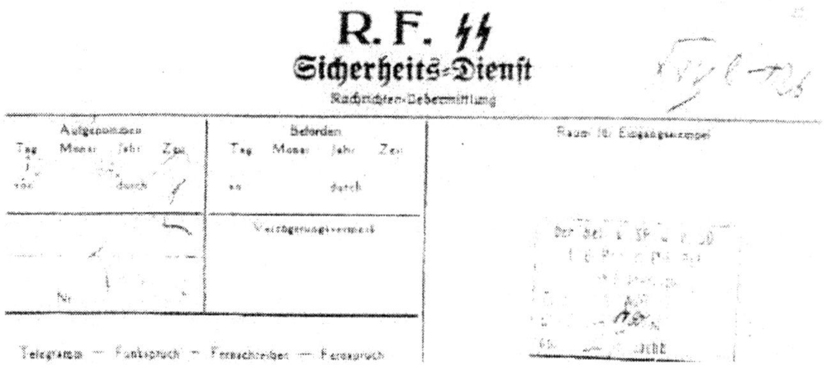

BERLIN AUGUST 13, 1942

SECRET-URGENT SUBJECT: TRANSPORT OF JEWS TO AUSCHWITZ WITH INCLUSION OF CHILDREN.

THE CHILDREN INTERNED IN THE CAMPS OF PITHIVIERS AND BEAUNE-LA-ROLANDE ARE TO BE DIVIDED OUT LITTLE BY LITTLE AMONG THE TRANSPORT TO AUSCHWITZ. IN ANY CASE, NO CONVOY IS TO TRANSPORT CHILDREN EXCLUSIVELY.

SIGNED: GUENTHERE, SSTRUMBANNFUHRER.

Archival telex of August 13, 1942: Secret-Urgent. (C.D.J.C.)

R.F. SS
Sicherheits-Dienst
Nachrichten-Uebermittlung

Aufgenommen — Tag Monat Jahr Zeit — von durch
Befördert — Tag Monat Jahr Zeit — an durch
Raum für Eingangsstempel
Verzögerungsvermerk
Nr.
Telegramm — Funkspruch — Fernschreiben — Fernspruch

BERLIN NUE 145 577 13.8.42 1617 =MA=
AN DEN BDS. DER SIPO UND DES SD IN BEREICH DES
MILITAERBEFEHLSHABERS IN FRANKREICH, PARIS. ==
G E H E I M -- DRINGEND. --
BETR.: ABRANSPORT VON JUDEN NACH AUSCHWITZ. DORT ABSCHUB
ABSCHUB DER JUDENKINDER. --
BEZUG: DORT. FS.-BERICHT V. 11.8.42 ROEM. 4 J. --
DIE IN DEN LAGERN PITHIVIERS UND BEAUNE-LA ROLANDE
UNTERGEBRACHTEN JUEDISCHEN KINDER KOENNEN NACH UND NACH
AUF DIE VORGESEHENEN TRANSPORTE NACH AUSCHWITZ AUFGETEILT
WERDEN. GESCHLOSSENE KINDERTRANSPORTE SIND JEDOCH
KEINENFALLS (UNTERSTR.) AUF DEN WEG ZU BRINGEN. --

-- RSHA. ROEM. 4 B 4 KL. 4 - [redacted] 3233/41 KL. - 6 (1085)
I.A. GEZ. GUENTHER SS-STUBAF. +

CHAPTER TWO

When There Was Peace

I was born in the beautiful city of Paris, France. Although my parents named me Sarah, they called me affectionately by my Yiddish/Jewish name, Sorele. My parents, my older sister Charlotte and I lived there very happily. My parents, Elie and Rhayke Pertzovsky, were originally from the shtetl (village) of Beltz in what was then Bessarabia and is now Moldavia. Having joined the many young Jews of their generation who were trying to escape the life of poverty their parents had led in the villages of the Pale of Settlement, provinces where Jews were allowed to live in what had been Czarist Russia, they were on their way to South America in 1925 when they found themselves stranded in Amsterdam. With the help of the Hebrew Immigrant Aid Society (H.I.A.S.), they were able to make their way to Paris, where they decided to settle. Soon after, my sister Charlotte was born, and by the time I was born five-and-a-half years later, my parents had established a new life in France.

Being enterprising people, my parents opened up a nice size beauty parlor where they both worked. At an early age I was aware of how long and hard they worked. Even so on that rare occasion that my mother had a little time to do chores in our apartment on the third floor of the same building as the beauty parlor, she would sing Yiddish folk songs in her sweet voice. I soon learned the beautiful melodies and words, which filled my heart and soul. Although I was born in France and I am profoundly fond of its language, I am sure that it was in such moment of heartfelt communication that my identity as the loving daughter of Jewish immigrants in the Diaspora took root.

Music was not my only passion. There was also school, I loved learning! I particularly remember the first lesson I had to learn by heart, how I repeated it almost to obsession, and my parents' approval when I was at last able to say, *"la ligne qui separe le ciel de la terre, s'appelle l'horizon. "The line that separates the sky from the earth is called the horizon."* There were surely good things on my horizon. I would continue the schooling that I loved so much and, maybe, one day I would become a singer, since I loved to sing and learned a lot of folk and popular songs from listening to the radio. Charlotte would most likely become a nurse or a doctor, because even at that age she was more interested in taking care of people than in going to school. And my parents would continue to work in their beauty parlor and would always be there for me when I came running home from school at the end of the day.

But as much as I loved school, I was always happy when the weekend came. On Sunday, a day of rest, we usually went to visit the Cogans—Aunt Perla, Maman's older sister, Uncle Avram, and their two sons, Volf and Georges—who had settled in Paris after my parents. Aunt Perla would bake wonderful *kugel* (noodle pudding) and *pletselech* (cookies) and Uncle Avram would fiddle Jewish melodies from his native Romania. What a *klezmech* (itinerant musician) he would have made! Cousin Volf, already a teenager, would play the piano, losing himself in Chopin's music while his older brother Georges would settle down with my father to a "serious game of chess." I, of course, would sing for the family as they sat around Aunt Perla's parlor drinking tea.

This photograph, taken just before the outbreak of the war in 1939, shows my sister Charlotte and me, ages fourteen and eight, and our cousins, Volf and Georges Cogan, ages fifteen and eighteen. It was meant to be sent to our grandparents in Russia, as was the yearly custom. (Photo coll.: Suzanne Gross)

Summertime was, if anything, even more idyllic. Every summer my parents would send me to the small village of Courchamps to spend a few months with the Demoncy family.

(Charlotte didn't go. She liked Paris better). Madame Demoncy had been the concierge in our Paris apartment building, and had often taken care of me while my parents were working in the beauty parlor. When Mr. Demoncy retired, he, his wife, and their young son Gerard moved to Mr. Demoncy's family home, nestled among the rich soil of this isolated village.

Although I missed my parents, I loved being in the beautiful countryside. I particularly remember Sunday morning in Courchamps. The Demoncys would dress up and go out to attend mass in the village's old church, which was on a small hill just to the right of their house. I usually slept late on Sundays and was awakened by the sound of the villagers coming out of services. I would open my bedroom shutters and gaze down on the graceful flower garden below my window. During the week, Mr. Demoncy, as I called him, tended the lovely garden from morning until night. Bordering the flower garden was another garden, this one filled with neat rows of vegetables, which would extend about forty yards from the house to turn and continue out of sight. Beyond was a low stone wall, and in the distance I could see rolling hills covered with resplendent red poppies swaying in the gentle breeze. Here and there, cows would graze on those slopes, or simply stand still in the summer heat under the shade offered by a few large old trees.

Behind the village church were a few graves, some dating back as far back as the eighteen hundreds. One tombstone, set apart, was mysteriously marked by a Star of David.

On one of my parents' visits, I remember, we put small stones on that grave, a Jewish practice showing that the grave had been visited. My mother had her picture taken near it, with a bunch of flowers in her hands, as if to acknowledge an abandoned and lonely Jewish soul.

In her younger days Madame Demoncy had been a cook for a Parisian family, so every part of making a meal was a big production in her house—even mashing potatoes. One had to beat and cook the potatoes again and again, and of course, my help was very much needed. On Fridays, because Catholics would always eat fish, Monsieur Demoncy would patiently remove all the bones from my fish so I could eat it without fear of choking.

In this virtual heaven on earth, there was much for us children to do. Along with other children from the village, Gerard and I would climb up and roll down high stacks of hay at one of the neighbor's farms. We would tease aggressive and noisy geese into running after us, and then scream in fear and delight as we ran away. Sometimes we would watch the women of the village do their wash in a stream, or sit by a shady pond covered with moss and watch frogs spring out as if they were putting on a show for us. Living with Monsieur and Madame Demoncy in the lovely countryside of Courchamps made my summers a very happy time, and taught me the true meaning of peace and love. It also gave me faith in the basic goodness of people that would sustain me in the difficult times ahead.

Mr. Demoncy, Mme. Demoncy, the family dog, Gerard and me, Sarah. (Photo coll.: Suzanne Gross)

Life in Paris was different, of course, but no less filled with love. One of my fondest memories is of the social evenings my family spent at a Jewish organization called the *Arbeiter Ring* (Workman's Circle). My parents would sometimes take my sister and me along to the gatherings where, with other children, we would sing Yiddish songs with the grown ups. (Although my parents had taken French lessons, Charlotte and I spoke French in school and with our little friends. My father and mother spoke Yiddish at home. We girls learned this expressive language as if by osmosis). These evenings were usually filled with gaiety, but occasionally there were heated discussions about someone called Hitler, a place called Germany, refugees, the Spanish Civil War, anti-Semitism, Poland and Russia...all this grown-up stuff! One of the other families that belonged to the *Arbeiter Ring* was that of my parent's friends and their son Michel. Originally from Poland, they now lived on *rue d'Avron* in a crowded blue-collar workers' quarter about a mile from where we lived.

Michel and I saw each other at the *Arbeiter Ring*, and also when he would accompany his father when he got his haircut at my parents' beauty parlor, as well as come with his mother when she had her hair done. It was during these visits that we developed a friendship that was marked by games and laughter—hide and seek and roller-skating as well as sharing books and doing homework together. On Thursdays, which we always had off from school, I would walk over to his place and spend time visiting with him, or he would come visiting with me. On special occasions we would be given a few *sous* (cents) and go to a movie with my big sister and her friends. Michel was also present at an important event in my young life. It was the first day of May, although I do not recall in what year, that Michel and I were given money by our fathers to get flowers for Mother's Day. It was the first time we were entrusted with buying presents, all by ourselves, for our mothers. I remember that we walked all over the neighborhood visiting flower shop after flower shop until we found the perfect flowers—Lilies of the Valley. I remember how appreciative my mother was of the gift—it meant so much to her.

That was the last time I saw my friend, Michel. One day I walked to his house, knocked on the door, and was met with an overwhelming silence. The little family had been taken away in a round up of Jews.

The store on the corner of rue des Haies and passage Dieu in Paris was once my parents' beauty parlor. Later on it became our place of hiding. This beauty parlor saved our lives.

Chapter Three

When There Was War

By the time my friend Michel and his family were taken away in a roundup of Jews, France had long since been overrun by the invading German army. The Nazis had invaded Poland in the fall of 1939, starting the war, and in the first six months of 1940 had attacked and rapidly conquered Denmark, Norway, Luxembourg, the Netherlands, Belgium, and my own beloved France.

On June 22, at Compiegne, in the same railroad car that German officials had surrendered in World War One, French officials were forced to sign an armistice with Germany, agreeing to disarm the French army and allow France to be divided into several sections. The two departments of Alsace and Lorraine, which had been part of Germany before the First World War became part of the Third Reich and the departments of the *Nord* and the *Pas-de-Calais* in northeastern France were put under the command of a German military governor based in Belgium.

The remaining area was divided between an occupied and an unoccupied zone. The occupied zone was also placed under the command of a German military governor, while the unoccupied zone was administered by a puppet government in Vichy under Marshall Philippe Petain, a French military hero of the First World War. Under the agreement, laws made in Vichy were to be applied to both the occupied and unoccupied zone, as long as they did not conflict with the policies of the German Government. Among the first laws that were passed, were those placing restrictions on Jews.

The purpose of these restrictions was to deprive Jews, using legalized anti-Semitism, of their means of existence, their freedom, and their participation in society. It began as soon as the Vichy government came to power. On July 16, the citizenship of naturalized Jews was revoked, and two days later Jews were barred from holding government positions or management posts in business and industry. But this was just the beginning. Between the summer of 1940 and the summer of 1943, the Vichy government issued a series of laws restricting Jewish involvement in French society in a variety of areas.

Residence: In May 1940, Jews were forbidden to move from one place of residence to another without official authorization.

Protection: In August 1940, the "Marchandeau Law" of 1939, which protected groups of people from racial and religious defamation and insults, was annulled, giving free rein to anti-Semitic propaganda.

Who is a Jew: In October 1940, it was declared that a Jew is any person descended from three grandparents of the Jewish "race" or from two grandparents if one's partner was also descended from two Jewish grandparents. This was the first introduction in French law of the notion of Jews as a "race" instead of a people who practiced Judaism. Later, in July 1941, it was decreed that anyone who had Jewish grandparents was to be considered a Jew.

Registration: Between October 3 and 19, 1940, all Jews were required to register with the police.

Citizenship: At the same time, the "Cremieux Decree," which had granted French Algerian Jews French nationality was annulled, and their French citizenship revoked.

Communication and Transportation: Also in 1940, in an effort to restrict the Jews ability to communicate or travel, they were required to turn into the police any radios, bicycles, cars or telephones.

Organizations: In November 1941, all Jewish organizations were dissolved and replaced by the *Union Generale des Israelites de France* (U.G.I.F.), which was to monitor and control the Jewish population. Membership in the U.G.I.F. was made mandatory for all Jews.

Curfew: Starting in February 1942, all Jews were required to be inside their homes between eight o'clock in the evening and six o'clock in the morning.

Children: In March 1942, a census was decreed for all French and foreign-born Jewish children under fifteen years of age.

Transportation: Also in June, all Jews traveling on subways were required to sit only in the last car.

Shopping: In July 1942, Jews were prohibited from shopping at any time other than between three and four o'clock in the afternoon.

Identity Papers: Starting in December 1942, the word *Juif* was to be stamped on every Jew's identity papers and ration cards.

Public Places: In August 1942, Jews were prohibited to be in public places such as libraries, playgrounds, museums, parks, movies, theaters, concert halls, public pools, beaches, etc.

Identification: Starting in June 1942, all Jews six years old or older were required to wear a yellow Jewish star, inscribed *Juif* (Jew), on their clothing.

Because he was a highly decorated, disabled war veteran, Victor Faynzilber was exempted from wearing the Jewish star required of all Jews over the age of six. Although his ten-year-old daughter wears the Star of David, his young son is not required to do so. Faynzilber was later deported to Auschwitz. (Photo: C.D.J.C.)

The sign on the fence reads: "PLAYGROUND, reserved for children, forbidden to Jews." (Photo:C.D.J.C.)

GENERAL INSPECTION OF LIBRARIES HM. -42-No. 6843-70-

Jews are forbidden access to public libraries THE PREFECT OF THE SEINE

Paris, October 9,1942

Notification #211

As of July 8, orders forbid Jews access to various public building, in particular public libraries.

Please inform the public of this measure by the means of a poster, hung in full view with the following text:

"Following the orders of July 8, 1942, access is forbidden to Jews." "Jewish

members of the library must return books taken out without delay."

From now on, when a new member subscribes to the library, the following certificate must be signed:

"I swear that I am not a Jew (or Jewess) as per the law of June 2, 1941, and that I do not have a Prefect identity card."

Paris, (to be dated)
(signature)

In case the reader has a new identity card, it must be shown so that the certificate can be modified as necessary.

In the libraries that have subscription members, the new members will have to write their own certificate on the back of their membership cards. For the libraries that have only a registry, the above guaranty will be written *in* the space reserved for the signature of the reader.

The General Inspector of Libraries:
(signature)

Order forbidding Jewish access to libraries. (C.D.J.C.)

INSPECTION GENERALE DES BIBLIOTHEQUES

Interdiction des Bibliothèques publiques aux Juifs

HM.-42-N°6843-70-

PREFECTURE DU DEPARTEMENT DE LA SEINE

Paris, le 9 Octobre 1942.

CIRCULAIRE N° 211

Des instructions du 8 Juillet ont interdit aux Juifs l'accès de divers édifices publics, notamment des bibliothèques.

Je vous prie de vouloir bien informer le public de cette mesure par l'affiche que vous apposerez, bien en évidence, à l'intérieur de la bibliothèque; elle sera libellée comme suit :

"En vertu des instructions du 8 Juillet 1942, l'accès des bibliothèques publiques est interdit aux Juifs."

" Les lecteurs juifs précédemment inscrits doivent rapporter, "dans le plus bref délai, les livres de la bibliothèque qu'ils possèderaient encore."

Dorénavant, lorsque vous procéderez à une inscription de lecteur, vous ferez souscrire l'attestation suivante :

"Je certifie sur l'honneur ne pas être Juif (ou Juive) aux termes de la loi du 2 Juin 1941 et n'être pas possesseur de la carte d'identité préfectorale".

Paris, le (à dater)

(Signature)

Dans le cas où le lecteur aurait la nouvelle carte d'identité, il devrait vous la présenter et vous modifieriez la fin de l'attestation en conséquence.

Pour les bibliothèques où il existe un fichier des lecteurs inscrits, les nouveaux lecteurs écriront eux-mêmes cette attestation au verso de la carte d'inscription. Pour celles où il n'existe qu'un registre, cette déclaration sera écrite sur le registre, dans le cadre réservé à la signature du lecteur.

L'INSPECTEUR GENERAL DES BIBLIOTHEQUES :

D. [illegible]

The restrictions placed on Jews were not only designed to limit their role in French society in general, they were also intended to limit the Jews' role in the nation's economic life. In order to keep the Germans from acquiring Jewish property, the French authorities initiated a policy that was referred to as "Aryanization." Aryanization, in the Nazi doctrine was the transfer of Jewish ownership of properties to non-Jewish Caucasians.

Intended to dispossess the Jewish population, this Aryanization was carried out through a series of laws passed between the summer of 1940 and the summer of 1941.

Starting in October 1940, a specially constituted police unit under the direction of Alfred Rosenberg* in Berlin seized works of art and other valuables from Jewish owners.

In September 1940, forced seizure of Jewish businesses with the appointment of "Aryan" administrators went into effect. Thousands of Jewish-owned businesses and properties were subjected to sell at low prices, to non-Jews.

Also in September 1940, any Jews who had run away from northern France as the Germans were invading the country were forbidden to return to their homes and businesses in the occupied zone.

In October 1940, all Jewish businesses were required to be registered with the Police and all Jewish shopkeepers were to put up a sign in their storefront windows reading *"Entreprise Juive"* ("Jewish business").

*Alfred Rosenberg, official Nazi ideologist of the Nazi party, was at first appointed by Hitler as High Commissioner of Education. He also conducted art-looting activities of the Einsatzstab Rosenberg in France, Belgium, the Netherlands, Luxembourg, Norway, Denmark, the occupied Eastern territories, Hungary and Greece. Documents show that he looted 71,000 Jewish homes. As late as 1944, the Rosenberg Ministry was overseeing the forced labor program and economic exploitation. Rosenberg was tried at the Nuremberg trials and was sentenced to death for crimes against humanity.

Storefront of a Jerwish-owned business with the sign obliatory after 1940 stating "Jewish ownership." (C.D.J.C.)

Starting in April and May 1941, funds from the forced sales of Jewish businesses were deposited and frozen in the bank account of Jewish owners. In June 1941, traveling salesmen and pushcart vendors (sellers of fruits, vegetables, notions and clothing) were required to turn in their merchant's licenses to the police. Laws were also passed that forbade or severely restricted Jews from practicing a number of professions, including those of physicians, lawyers, government officials, pharmacists, professors, publicists, dentists, architects, teachers, travel agents, surgeons, and actors.

One of the major means by which Vichy tried to separate the Jews of France from the non-Jews was the establishment, on November 29, 1941, of the *Union Generale des Israelites de France* (U.G.I.F.). Although subordinate to Vichy's *"Commissariat des Questions Juives,"* the U.G.I.F. was ultimately under the power and the authority of *SS Hauptsturmfuhrer* Theodor Dannecker, Chief of the Gestapo's Jewish Office in France, among whose responsibilities was the deportation of Jews. Leaders of the Jewish organizations that had been disbanded by the Gestapo were pressured to take charge of the U.G.I.F.

The U.G.I.F. was formed to represent Jews in matters of public assistance, mutual aid and social re-adaptation. And it did in fact help people in need in a variety of ways, including, among other things, creating children's homes for orphans whose parents were deported. In reality, however, the organization was a double-edged sword, though it did provide valuable assistance, it also allowed the French police and the Gestapo to monitor and control the Jewish population. For example, at one point it was ordered to conduct a census of the entire Jewish population, which was in turn used to hunt the Jews. Later, the organization was also required to collect a fine of one billion francs from the Jewish community as a reprisal for an attack upon German soldiers by the Resistance.

Although those who worked for the U.G.I.F. consistently tried to help their Jewish compatriots, their efforts were ultimately doomed to failure. For example, later in the war, after Raymond-Raoul Lambert, the head of the organization in southern France, protested the inhumane treatment of the Jewish population to French President Laval, he was deported to Auschwitz along with his wife, Simone, and their four children—Lionel, fourteen; Marc, eleven; Tony, four and Marie France, eighteen months. His counterpart in northern France suffered a similar fate. After complaining to Laval of the sadistic behavior of *SS Hauptstfuhrer* Alois Bruner toward Jews interned in the camp at Drancy, Andre Baur and his wife, Odette, were also deported with their children—Pierre, ten; Miriam, nine; Antoine, six and Francine, three. No Lambert or Baur family member was ever seen again.

Raymond-Raoul Lambert, head of the U.G.I.F. in Southern France, his wife, Simone, and their four children—Lionel, Marc, Tony, and Marie France. All were deported to Auschwitz in December 1943 (C.D.J.C.).

Chapter Four

Through the Cracks in the Shutters

Like all "Jewish" businesses, my parents' beauty parlor had to be registered in the police census of October 1940 and they had to put a sign in the window reading "Entreprise Juive." Because subsequent anti-Jewish laws promulgated by the French government forbade Jews to have contact with the public, eventually the beauty parlor had to be closed. Suddenly, from one day to the next, my parents could not make a living. I felt their sadness. All the windows were covered with shutters except for a small upper window above the street entrance. One day the French police came to apply thick wax seals on the back entrance door, so no one would be able to go in. Nevertheless, to enter the beauty parlor there was a concealed trap door in the cellar through which you could get inside. And the gate to the cellar was located along the hallway with a tiled floor that made it possible to hear if some one was outside before you tried to get out.

By that time, foreign Jewish refugees were already interned in camps such as Gurs and Rivesaltes, and it was then that my parents determined that "it would be best to run… to hide…to make them work to try to catch us!" Since the French police would bang on the door most often in the wee hours of the night to take away Jewish men, considering that the beauty parlor appeared closed and sealed, it was decided that if the police were to come for my father, they would not look for him there. Therefore it would be a safer place for him to sleep than in our apartment upstairs.

My father installed a table on which he put several old cardboard advertisements around a small candle, so the light could not be detected outside. Daddy slept on a mattress on the floor. Within a few months, my mother, my sister and I joined him each night so he would not be alone. In the early morning hours we would return upstairs to our apartment. For a ten-year-old, this situation felt surreal, as it would for any child. It seemed as if my family and I were living a double life—in a way we were. School, though, was my salvation because there I felt that I was like all the children. Eventually that, too, would be taken away.

Our shop was at one end of the block, angled in such a way that the police station could be seen at the other end. Our street-level, corner location, where I could "spy" on outside life through some cracks in the shutters in almost three directions, saved me for a while from my worst enemy—the weight of aimless time. It also meant that we were the first to see or hear the activities at the police station.

Eventually, of course, the French police came for us. We were downstairs, hiding in the shuttered and sealed store, and there they were upstairs banging loudly on the door of our apartment! It woke us up in the middle of the night. We waited frozen and silent in the cruel darkness. Three times they came for us, and each time Madame Blanchard, our concierge, told them, "I have not seen them for a long time." Her courage and her humanity, time and time again, saved us.

Because she was so determined to save us, and so faithful in that determination, Madame Blanchard took on larger than life dimensions for me. I was filled with admiration and esteem for her. Who would have believed that this unassuming, gray-haired, middle-aged lady, who I would see delivering the mail day in and day out, whom I would greet with a quick "*bonjour* Madame Blanchard" and who would answer with a silent nod and smile, could have possessed such selfless courage? I thought, as my Aunt Perla had told me the story of a *Lamedvovnick,* (a righteous person) that for sure she was a *Lamedvovnick*. In Jewish folklore, based in part on the Babylonian Talmud, there are thirty-six anonymous righteous men in every generation, each of whom is called a *Lamedvovnick (lamed* and *vav* are the two Hebrew letters which together represent the number thirty six.) These "Hidden Saints" are responsible for the fate of this world. Normally they go unnoticed by other men because of their humble nature and vocation. But in times of danger they make dramatic appearances, use their hidden powers to defeat the enemies of Israel, and then return to the anonymity from which they came.

But Madame Blanchard was not the only one who was willing to risk her own life to help us. My father's friend, Chaouche, was also a *Lamedvovnick*. He was from the French colony of Algeria in North Africa and like many of his compatriots, lived alone in Paris without his family. Most Algerians who stayed in France worked hard in menial jobs, such as road or building construction. A devout Muslim, soft spoken and quick to smile, Chaouche must have understood the hardship of being an outcast in

French society. Each month, he took it upon himself to get our ration tickets, which were tucked into a booklet stamped *Juif* in red. Although the bureaucratic maze of Jewish registrations was designed to catch every Jew, for some reason it yet didn't work in this case. Incredibly, he was never stopped and questioned.

In fact, getting food while in hiding was a daily preoccupation. Food was scarce and rationed in German-occupied France, so you had to be lucky, under our circumstances of living in hiding, in order to get a meal. Additionally, Jews were limited to shopping only between three and four o'clock in the afternoon. This was a problem because a grocery store would advertise the arrival of potatoes—or some other food—for the next day, and people would start lining up at six o'clock in the morning. But the few hours Jews had to shop did not permit hours of queuing. There was also the added burden of wearing the Star of David, which could expose you to hostility or denunciation. You could hide the Star of David, but you ran a serious risk if the police came and started checking identity papers. Scenes of fear and frustration would repeatedly occur when my sister Charlotte, who was then about fifteen or sixteen years old, would be on her way to try to get food.

My fearful mother would caution her " not to show her Star of David while waiting in line...but to show it half way, just in case...to cover it and try to get away if necessary," My poor sister would vent her frustration as quietly as she could.

Because of these restrictions we were hungry all the time and sometimes I did not feel well. Madame Blanchard would visit us very late at night and bring us hot soup or stew.

Chaouche would also occasionally show up with some food. And after my father joined the Resistance, he would sneak in food for us. There were also some soup kitchens organized by the U.G.I.F. Yet, it was best to avoid those soup kitchens, because such places, where many Jews would gather, were in imminent danger of possible roundups. But hunger drove us out. When we went, we would always walk, although it was quite far, because the subways—where Jews were restricted to ride only in the last car of the train—could be another trap.

Through all this I would daydream of Aunt Perla's *kugels*; of the warm mashed potatoes that I used to whip up to help my mother; the chicken my mother served for *Shabbos* dinner; and of the crusty croissants my sister Charlotte and I would pick up after school at the neighborhood bakery. I would also think with regret about the food I had left on my plate when it was plentiful.

CHAPTER FIVE

The Green Police Warrant

It was May 14, 1941 when, like many Jewish men, our neighbor, Monsieur Sender, had received a green warrant to come to the police station that very day. He went with Marcel, his fourteen year old son, who later came back to fetch some clothes and toilet articles for his father. Because the station was visible from our apartment windows, we could see that it was surrounded by French police with rifles. We could also see the continuous arrival and departure of buses filled with men. As we later learned, Monsieur Sender was one of the 3,747 Jewish men arrested that day. We never saw him again.

While I watched what was going on across the street, Mother and Father kept running next door to the Senders' apartment. Mother was bringing food to them. Later as I stood in the hallway, through the slightly opened door I could see Madame Sender sitting, bent over and sobbing. Marcel, with tears streaming down his face, was trying to comfort her. Later still when I passed by their door, I had an empty feeling and a gnawing thought entered my mind: What if "they" were to take my father away too? Monsieur Sender would be the first of many neighbors and acquaintances who would be taken. It was confusing and frightening. How could a person having done no wrong be removed from his family, from his work, from his daily life? Stores of Jewish owners kept closing—the only Jewish grocery in the neighborhood, a stationary and printing shop, a shoe store, a furniture shop. The Jewish community was disappearing. My parents said that our non-Jewish neighbors were watching what was happening to the Jews in silence and going about their lives as though nothing was happening. Is that what war did to people—make them indifferent? Didn't they care what was happening to us?

We soon learned that the men who had been taken away were being detained in what was called a *camp de concentration,* a "concentration camp." One was located in the town of Pithiviers and another in Beaune-la-Rolande. But as more Jewish men were rounded up in Paris during the month of August, a new camp was established in Drancy, a suburb of the capital. Although we had no way of knowing it at the time, Drancy would become the last stop before the deportation to the death camps in the "East."

The first one in my family to be incarcerated in Drancy was my cousin Georges, who had been taken in the August roundups. I remember making a few trips on Sundays to see him there. Although I was accompanied, I do not remember who went with me. What I do remember is that there were a great many people filling the streets surrounding the camp, all trying to see into the large picture windows in the camp's buildings—the glimpse of a father, a son, a grandfather, an uncle, a cousin, a friend or a neighbor. It was hard to see from the street where we were, even though the imprisoned men seem excited by our presence. It hurt to see all those innocent Jewish men imprisoned. We cared so much. We heard all kinds of frenzied rumors: the men went hungry, there were suicides and some men had been liberated—but who and why? As punishment, some had been thrown in a hole.

There was a resistance movement in the camp. A woman in the street was arrested because she was sending messages by tracing words in the air with a stick. Other people in the street had been arrested, some for no apparent reason. A lot of the rumors turned out to be true. Then one Sunday we went to Drancy only to find all the windows painted blue! We could no longer see the men. But even though that had been taken away from us, there still seemed to be a kind of silent human reverberation emanating from the buildings. After this happened, we no longer visited on Sundays.

Because of the dire conditions in Drancy, in the first few months after the camp opened there were a great many deaths among the prisoners. Fearful of an epidemic, on the recommendation of a French and German medical commission on May 5 and 6, 1941, officials released 750 morbidly ill men from the camp. One of them was my cousin Georges, who was in a pitiful state. He was malnourished and so wasted that he was like a walking skeleton. After his release he did not speak for months and even afterwards he never spoke of what he had experienced there. It was as if what he had suffered and seen was between him and God. Although he would survive, it would affect him for the rest of his life.

Pithiviers, Beaune-la-Rolande, and Drancy were all part of a system of camps that, under the imminent threat of war in the late 1930s, the French

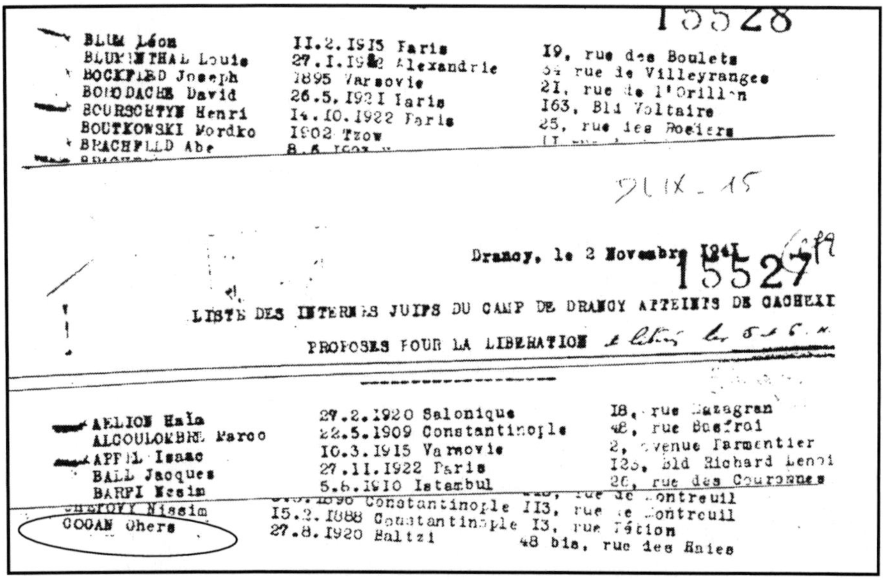
15528

BLUM Léon	11.2.1915 Paris	19, rue des Boulets
BLUMENTHAL Louis	27.1.1912 Alexandrie	54 rue de Villeyranges
BOCKFIED Joseph	1895 Varsovie	21, rue de l'Orillon
BONDDACHE David	26.5.1921 Paris	163, Bld Voltaire
BOURSCHTYN Henri	14.10.1922 Paris	25, rue des Rosiers
BOUTKOWSKI Mordko	1902 Tzow	[illegible]
BRACHFELD Abe	[illegible]	

21 IX - 15

Drancy, le 2 Novembre 1941 15527

LISTE DES INTERNES JUIFS DU CAMP DE DRANCY ATTEINTS DE CACHEXIE PROPOSES POUR LA LIBERATION

AELION Haim	27.2.1920 Salonique	18, rue [illegible]
ALCOULOMBRE Marco	22.5.1909 Constantinople	48, rue Beffroi
APPEL Isaac	10.3.1915 Varsovie	2, avenue Parmentier
BALL Jacques	27.11.1922 Paris	125, Bld Richard Lenoir
BARPI Nesim	5.6.1910 Istambul	26, rue des Couronnes
[illegible] Nissim	[illegible] Constantinople	113, rue de Montreuil
COGAN Ghers	15.3.1888 Constantinople	13, rue Pétion
	27.8.1920 Baltzi	48 bis, rue des Haies

Archival partial list showing that **my cousin Georges**, listed at the very bottom under his name "**Cogan Ghers**," was released on November 5 or 6, 1941. The first convoy to the death camp of Auschwitz left Paris/le Bourget, March 27, 1942. (Jojo Cogan coll.)

had built or converted to hold any "undesirable" foreigners who might flee to France from their native countries. One of the first of these camps was the one at Gurs, in southern France near the Spanish border. It was one of eight such camps created in the winter and spring of 1938 for refugees and soldiers from the International Brigades who had been fighting Francisco Franco and his Nationalists in the Spanish Civil War.

Gurs was flooded with another kind of refugee—German and Austrian Jews—men, women and children who had found refuge in France and were arrested in late November 1939 by the French after their declaration of war with Germany. Because of the enormous influx, even though the camp at Gurs had been built to hold only fifteen thousand people, eventually eighteen thousand men, women and children were detained there. Not only was the camp overcrowded, but also food was scarce and the living conditions in general were deplorable. As a result, within a few months of the German Jews' arrival there, and despite efforts by a variety of charitable organizations, nearly fourteen hundred people died of starvation, dysentery, and typhus.

The French internment camp at Gurs (Photo C.DJ.C.)

Jewish infants in the French internment camp at Gurs. (C.D.J.C.)

Mealtime at the camp at Gurs. Soup was the main dietary staple at Gurs, as at many other camps. Because camp inmates were not provided with the basic utensils needed for eating, acquiring a container for one's meal became a necessity for survival. (Photo: C.D.J.C.)

Another one of the camps was Rivesaltes. Also in the south of France, near the Pyrenees, Rivesaltes had originally been established as a transit camp for colonial troops during the First World War. Nicknamed the "Sahara of the South" because of its extremely hot summers and icy winters, it was a particularly inhospitable location. This, in addition to the lack of basic sanitation as well as inadequate medical care, led to severe malnutrition among many of the camp's inmates, particularly children.

In fact, on July 9, 1941, a petition to camp officials from the heads of the camp barracks complained, "Most of the children refuse to eat the soup made of turnips and the exterior leaves of cabbages...[and] as a result many of the children are weakened physically and emotionally listless." But the petition did little good. During the months of August and September 1941, of the 140 young children in Rivesaltes, sixty of them perished. Fortunately, by January 1942, private organizations succeeded in having most of the children released from the camp.

Jewish children in the camp of Rivesaltes (C.D.J.C.)

From the time that the first police warrants were received, there had been bewilderment in the community. According to shocking—and unbelievable rumors—not only were the French rounding up Jews for the Germans, but also they were shipping them to special camps in the "East" that had been built particularly to keep Jewish prisoners. Even more difficult to believe, the Germans were said to be experimenting with killing people in gas vans in the woods. The gas vans were filled with Jews!

Chapter Six

Restrictions and Resistance

Although the world would not learn of this for several years, on January 20, 1942, a group of high-ranking Nazi officials gathered for a meeting at a villa in the Berlin suburb of Wannsee. The group had been charged by Adolph Hitler with working out plans for what was referred to as the "Final Solution" to the Jewish question. The solution they arrived at that day—the extermination of the Jewish people—would have ramifications across Europe and ultimately, around the entire world. While we of course knew nothing about this meeting, the actions that the Vichy government had taken against the Jews of France had nevertheless made it increasingly clear that Vichy—and the Nazi masters—had already declared war on the Jews.

My father was particularly aware of this. After my parents had closed the beauty parlor, he had gone to work for a short time in the steel factory of Schmit and Sons. There was a lot of unhappiness in the family about his working conditions there—he worked near the fire and would often come home burned. It was there that he met Chaouche, who later would contribute so much to our survival. It was there too, that he learned about the Underground Resistance. The factory was part of the German war machine, but many of the workers were part of the Resistance, and my father got to know some of them. Eventually he decided that he had to fight back, and left the factory to join the underground Jewish Brigade, which would later be known as "*Companie Rayman.*"

The company was named after a young Jewish hero who had been a member of this Jewish Partisan Unit and who had been tortured and killed by the Nazis. The unit had carried out numerous acts of sabotage in and around Paris between March 1942 and November 1943. Among these were:

- Bomb and hand-grenade attacks on sixty-two hotels.
- Arson of fifteen German recruiting offices, sixteen garages, and seventy eight work-shops and warehouses containing war material.
- Destruction of one hundred and twenty three buses and two anti-aircraft guns.
- Hand-grenade attacks on nineteen busloads of Nazis, thirty-one military groups, seventeen groups of German officers, and seventeen military barracks.
- Assassination of SS General Julius Ritter, who was responsible for deporting hundreds of thousands of Frenchmen to Germany for slave labor.
- Killing of four additional high-ranking officers and eleven traitors.

(From They Fought Back by Yuri—N.Y. Schocken, 1967/1975)

"Companie Rayman," a Jewish Partisan Unit of *Franc-Tireurs et Partisans-Main-d'Oeuvre Immigres* (FTP-MOI). My father, Eli Pertzovsky, is the man wearing a beret, seated four from the left in the third row. (Photo: Suzanne Gross collection)

While some Jews joined the Companie Rayman to resist the Germans, others had to survive whether in hiding or not. My cousin Georges who had been released from the Drancy concentration camp, went back to work despite his poor health and he got a job with a construction company. Because he was a Jew, he could work only if he had no contact with the public, and had to have a special certificate from his employer to prove it.

CERTIFICATE

We the undersigned CUSOL EST'OUP and Company, Builders, 57 rue Rennequin, Paris 17, declare that we have hired Mr. Cogan Georges on the 13th of March, N42, at an hourly rate of 11. frs 10.

Mr. Cogan, who is an Israelite, does not have any contact with the public in his work.

Paris,6 May 1942
CUSOL ESTOUP AND COMPANY

(Stamped by the Police Station of the 17th Paris District 8 May 1942)

My Cousin Georges Cogan's Certificate of employment, May 1942.
(Photo: collection of Jojo Cogan)

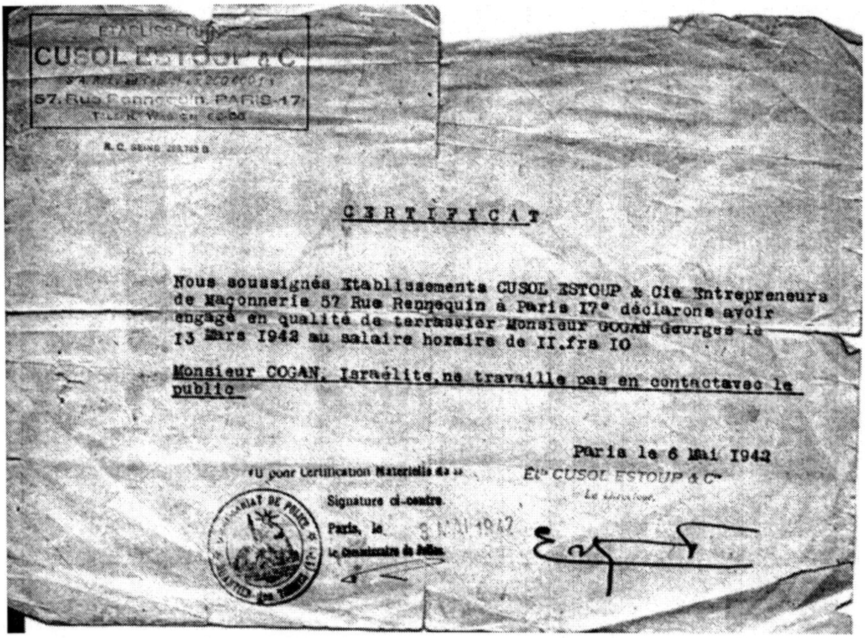

CUSOL ESTOUP & C
57 Rue Rennequin PARIS 17

CERTIFICAT

Nous soussignés Etablissements CUSOL ESTOUP & Cie Entrepreneurs de Maçonnerie 57 Rue Rennequin à Paris 17e déclarons avoir engagé en qualité de terrassier Monsieur COGAN Georges le 13 Mars 1942 au salaire horaire de II.frs IO

Monsieur COGAN, Israélite,ne travaille pas en contactavec le public

Paris le 6 Mai 1942
Ets CUSOL ESTOUP & Cie

Vu pour Certification Matérielle de la
Signature ci-contre
Paris, le 8 MAI 1942
Le Commissaire de Police

Nothing was as it had been. We knew that, as Jews, we had been set apart from the people of France. And if we could have by some chance forgotten, there were always new restrictions to remind us. I particularly remember on the night of May 28, 1942 my mother sewing a Star of David on my school dress by candlelight in the beauty parlor, where we already slept in hiding during the nights. As she sewed, she asked me how I felt about having to wear it out in the street as well as in school the next day? She thought that I might not want to go to school and just stay home and get used to the idea.

Or, she asked, did I perhaps want her to walk me to school? I was still very confused about what was going on. I could tell that my mother was worried about my first day at school wearing the Star of David, but I did not understand why. Even though her fear weakened my sense of courage, I told her not to worry. I was proud to wear the Star of David. And besides, I had friends in school. And I was Sarah—star or no star.

So the next day, my heart pounding with anticipation, I walked to school and entered the schoolyard where all the children were playing. Some of my friends came over, staring at my Star of David. Then more and more girls circled around me. I froze. No one said anything, until at one point a voice yelled out, *"Sale Juive!" ("Dirty Jewess!")* Overwhelmed with hurt and anger, I pushed my way out of the small crowd and ran sobbing to the principal. Taking me into her arms, she held me and rocked me gently. Later that day, a few of the teachers came into the classroom to peek at me. I remember their body language—some simply walked away, but there was one teacher who shook her head in disbelief. I was the only Jew in my class. And because I wore a star, even though I was the same Sarah, someone had taunted me as a "dirty Jewess." From that day on, my small happy world was gone.

Chapter Seven

"Spring Wind"

The Vichy government started rounding up Jewish men for deportation as early as spring of 1941, but it was not until the summer of 1942 that they began rounding up women and children as well. This operation, which was given the code name *"Vent Printanier" ("Spring Wind")*, was planned jointly by the SS and the French government, and carried out solely by the French police. It was expected to result in the capture of up to twenty-two thousand Jews and was part of the Nazis' overall plan to remove all the Jews from France and, ultimately deliver them to the death camps that were already established in the "East"—that is Poland and Germany.

According to telexes sent in early July by *SS Hauptsturmfuhrer* Theodor Dannecker in Paris to the Central Security Office in Berlin, it had already been decided that all the "Stateless Jews" in both the occupied and unoccupied part of France, that is, those whose citizenship had been revoked in Nazi controlled countries and had been living in France, would be rounded up for deportation. French President Laval seized the opportunity to get rid of thousands of Jewish refugees.

According to a telex sent by Dannecker on July 6 (pgs. 8-9), "He offered the Jews from the unoccupied zone, including children under sixteen years of age, to be taken along" to concentration camps. Nor was Laval concerned about any other children. In the same telex, Dannecker said of Laval, "The question of Jewish children left alone in the occupied zone is of no interest to him." The *hauptsturnfuhrer* accordingly asked to be allowed to start including children in the roundups and deportations. In a subsequent telex, this one sent on July 10 (pgs. 10-11), Dannecker also asked if the children of both the stateless—the French and foreign Jews living in France—could also be deported with the adults.

R.F. SS
Sicherheits-Dienst
Nachrichten-Uebermittlung

Aufgenommen Tag Monat Jahr Zeit von durch	Befördert Tag Monat Jahr Zeit 18 JUIL 1942 durch	Raum für Eingangsstempel
Nr.	Verzögerungsvermerk	
Telegramm — Funkspruch — Fernschreiben — Fernspruch		

Paris, July 18,1942

To the Central Security Office of the Reich
-IVB4-
B e r l i n

Subject: The Arrest of Stateless Jews by the French Police

The arrests were executed by the French police on the 16th and 17th of July 1942. Altogether, the people who were arrested can be divided as follows:

a) Men: 3,031
b) Women: 5,802
c) Children 4,051
Total 12,884

Six thousand men and women, single or without children, were immediately taken to Drancy internment camp, from where they will be deported to work camps in the Reich by trains, each with one thousand persons, within two weeks. The rest of the Jews arrested, especially women and children, have been taken to the Jewish camps of Beaune-la-Rolande and Pithiviers.

No decision has been taken concerning the possibility of deporting the children to the Reich. The care and food necessary for the arrested Jews are the French authority's responsibility.

Signed: Lischka
SS Obersturmbarmflihrer

Telex from SS Hauptsturmfuhrer Theodor Dannecker in Paris to the Central Security Office in Berlin, July 18, 1942. (C.D.J.C.)

R.F. SS
Sicherheits-Dienst
Nachrichten-Uebermittlung

Aufgenommen Tag Monat Jahr Zeit von durch	Befördert Tag Monat Jahr Zeit 18 JUIL 1942 an durch	Raum für Eingangsstempel
1192 Nr.	Verzögerungsvermerk	
Telegramm — Funkspruch — Fernschreiben — Fernspruch		

IV J - SA 225 n   Paris, den 18.7.1942

..h./Ge.

An das

Reichssicherheitshauptamt

- IV D 4 -

Berlin.

betrifft: Festnahme von staatenlosen Juden durch die französische Polizei

Vorgang: ohne.

Die von der französischen Polizei am 16. und 17.7.1942 durchgeführte Festnahmeaktion von staatenlosen Juden hat folgendes Ergebnis erbracht:

a) Männer 3 031

b) Frauen 5 802

c) Kinder 4 051

Insgesamt 12 884

Die kinderlosen Juden sind in dem Internierungslager Drancy untergebracht worden und werden mit den nächsten Transporten laufend abgeschoben. Die übrigen festgenommenen Juden werden mit den Kindern zunächst den Judenlagern Beaune-la-Rolande und Pithiviers zugeführt.

Da bei der Festnahmeaktion eine beträchtliche Anzahl Kinder mit festgenommen wurde und sich hinsichtlich der Unterbringung auf längere Dauer Schwierigkeiten ergeben, wird nochmals um Entscheidung gebeten, ob die Kinder mit den nächsten Transporten abgeschoben werden können.

I.V.

SS-Obersturmführer

PHOTO:
Collection Su

Although we of course had no knowledge of any of this, on July 16 we saw the results. Around four o'clock in the morning we were awakened by cries. Through the cracks in the shutters of the beauty parlor where we were sleeping, we could see both men and women carrying children and bundles going into the police station. At one point there were so many people that many stood around outside surrounded by French policemen with rifles.

In fact the entire operation was handled by French policemen. There was not a single German soldier in sight. As time went by the crowd became restless and there were cries for food and drinks. At about ten o'clock buses started to take the people away. Seeing this, my mother began to pace back and forth crying in Yiddish, *"Nebach! Goteniu! Zey nemen di kinder…di muters! Zey hobn guevern…zey kenen sheesn! (Pity! My God! They are taking the children…the mothers! They are armed…they can shoot!")* We were spared this time around, but this pitiful, immense roundup went on for two days.

From another telex sent on July 18 (pgs. 44-45), this one from an *SS Obersturmbannfuhrer* Lischka to the Central Security Office in Berlin, we know that in addition to 3,031 men, the police rounded up for the first time 5,802 women, and 4,051 children.

Couples without children were incarcerated in the Drancy concentration camp, while those with children were brought to the Vel d'Hiv, a vast indoors arena used for bicycle races in the summer and boxing matches in the winter. The summer heat, the over-crowding, and the lack of food, water, and sanitary facilities created bedlam and misery.

Diarrhea and dysentery spread among the people and unbearable odors began to pervade the place. The utter human neglect that the Jews would suffer had started. But it was just the beginning of their agony.

CHAPTER EIGHT

In the Transit Camps

Even while families were being rounded up, efforts were being made to rescue Jews—particularly Jewish children—from arrest, internment, and deportation. Several Jewish organizations and individuals, with the courageous help of some Christians, formed clandestine networks to save both children and adolescents. Among these were some of today's still familiar names such as the American Jewish Joint Distribution Committee and Refugee Aid, H.I.A.S or Hebrew Immigrant Aid Society, O.S.E. (Organization to Rescue Children or *Oeuvre de Secours aux Enfants*). They contributed to the support of imperiled Jews throughout Europe in a variety of ways during the dark and dangerous days of the Holocaust.

The E.I.F. or *Eclaireurs Israelites de France* (French Jewish Scouts) also provided the release of children and adolescents from the overcrowded French camps and created children's homes and work training centers. *Le circuit Garel* (the Garel Group), backed by a Catholic group led by a Jesuit, Father Pierre Chaillet, and the Abbe Glasberg (a former Jew who had converted and became a Catholic priest), helped by leading children to safety across the Swiss border. There were individual Christians, too, who tried to help the Jews. Catholic Archbishop Pierre Saliege broke the silence of his church by having a pastoral letter read in every church in his archdiocese condemning the "Spring Wind" arrests and stating that the Jews were "our brothers." Pastor Marc Boegner, president of the Federation of Protestant churches went to Vichy in an effort to save the children and the adolescents to no avail.

Many of the families who were initially brought to the Vel d'hiv in the July roundups were subsequently transported to the camps at Pithiviers and Beaune-la-Rolande. All these organizations tried to rescue as many children as they could from those camps.

The group Shema Israel, part of the *Eclaireurs Israelites de France* (French Jewish Scouts), helped the U.G.I.F. Center on rue Lamark care night and day for the children taken from internment after the "Spring Wind" arrests. (C.D.J.C.)

They also took on responsibility for many children whose parents were in hiding like me or had been deported, and, when possible, placed them in Christian homes and institutions, or with peasants on their farms in the country. Most of the people who accepted these children received some money—usually a minimum amount—to take care of them.

The fate of those children who were not so fortunate as to be rescued was very different. Like their parents, they were under a death sentence. The Nazis were determined to deport all the Jews of France to camps in the "East," where they would be systematically murdered. But in the summer of 1942, they were still working out the logistics of their plan. One of the questions that was still open was whether or not children would be deported with their parents.

Shortly before the roundups began, on July 1, during a meeting with *SS Obersturmbann-Fuhrer* Adolph Eichmann, *SS Hauptsturmfuhrer* Theodor Dannecker, chief of the Gestapo's Jewish Office in France, argued that the children should be deported with their parents. Even so, by July 31, 1942, permission to deport the children had not yet come from Berlin, so the French police began deporting mothers without their children.

According to a report filed with the French Committee of the Red Cross in London, when the women in *Beaune-la-Rolande* resisted separation from their children, French police forcibly separated them by beating both mothers and children with truncheons. As a result of the decision to deport the mothers separately, about thirty three hundred children—eighteen hundred in Pithiviers and fifteen hundred in Beaune-la-Rolande—were left there under the minimal supervision of social workers. Many of the children were in distress, suffering not only from the loss of their parents but also from malnutrition and dysentery.

One of the many families affected by this was the Gleisers. Three members of the family—mother, father, and nine-year-old daughter Annette—were among those arrested on July 16 and held at the Vel d'Hiv. At the time, Annette's brother Marcel was in the hospital recovering from an appendectomy, and her sister Therese was at work, which saved them both. The day after their arrests Annette's father was sent to Drancy camp, but she and her mother were sent to Pithiviers. A little more than a week later, on July 25, 1942, Annette's mother was deported, leaving the nine-year old on her own. While still in the camp, Annette asked her friend Maurice to write a letter on her behalf to her brother and sister. It was, in effect, her last contact. She and both her parents were transported to Auschwitz where all three perished.

Annette Gleiser, one of the four thousand children rounded up by the Nazis in July 1942, and sent to the camp at Pithiviers. (Marcel Gleiser Collection).

Annette Gleiser's mother was separated from her daughter on July 25, 1942. Mothers were taken away to complete the quotas of no less than 1000 Jews per deportation train.
(Marcel Gleiser Collection).

Annette Gleiser's father was transferred to Drancy Camp, last stop before his deportation, on July 17, 1942.

1942

Dear Therese and Marcel,

I am writing this letter with the help of Maurice Elef…Mama left July 25th for an "unknown destination" and also Papa on July 17th. I am now in good health, because I was in the infirmary with a sore throat. Maurice is watching over me. I would like you to send me a package of food. A little bit of sugar, biscottes, azyme bread, fruits, and also a cup; no can food. Send me stationary and envelopes. I like to know if you received my letter. I hope Marcel is in good health. On August 15, there was a departure of children and women for Drancy where Papa was. But I'm still here with Maurice, Marius and Paulette. Put some marmalade inside the cup and send me a small piece of soap. I end my Letter kissing you with all my heart, you and Marcel. I, Maurice, am writing a few words for Marcel. I am in the same barrack as your sister. All the children between 4 and 18 years of age had their hair shaved. I also send you kisses with all my heart. Say Hello to Mme S……, to Mme B…, and to Mme Richard.

Marcel, please tell Mme Merle that I sent her a letter asking for a package and if she did not get my letter to send it to me at the same address as Annette's

Maurice for
Annette Gleiser

Destination
Annette Gleiser M.34
Baraque N.c-campN.3
Pithiviers
Loiret

Annette is still in the same barrack.

The letter from Annette, from the camp of Pithiviers that was written in her behalf by her friend Maurice to her brother Marcel and her sister Therese.

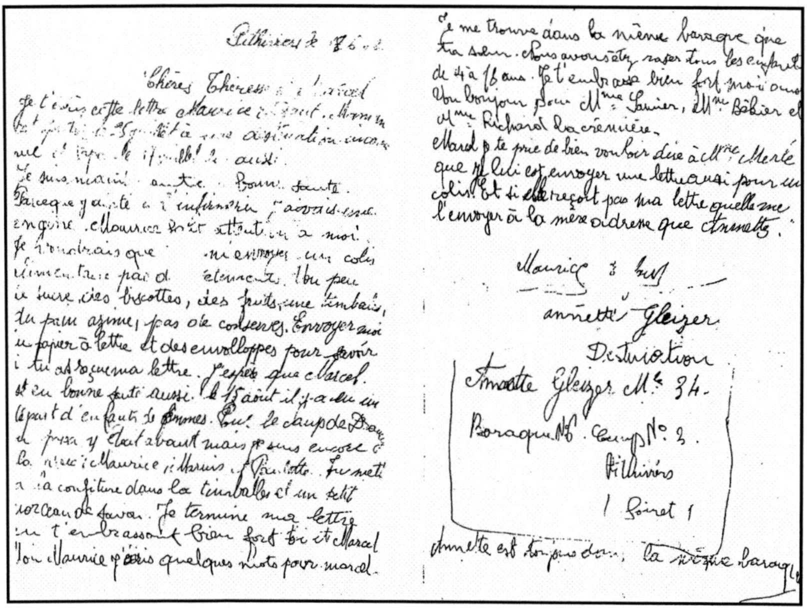

Pithiviers le [illegible]

Chères Therese [illegible] Marcel
Je t'écris cette lettre [illegible] Maurice [illegible]. Maman [illegible] à une destination incon[illegible]
[illegible] aussi.
Je suis [illegible] Bonne santé.
Parceque j'a[illegible] à l'infirmerie j'avais une
angine. Maurice [illegible] attention à moi.
Je voudrais que [illegible] m'envoyer un colis
[illegible] pas [illegible]. Un peu
de sucre, des biscottes, des fruits, une timbale,
du pain azime, pas de conserves. Envoyer moi
du papier à lettre et des envelloppes pour savoir
si tu as reçu ma lettre. J'espère que Marcel
est en bonne santé aussi. Le 15 août il y a eu un
départ d'enfants et femmes. [illegible] le camp de Drancy
[illegible] y était avant mais je suis encore
là [illegible] Maurice, Marius, [illegible] Paulette. [illegible]
[illegible] confiture dans la timballe et un petit
morceau de savon. Je termine ma lettre
en t'embrassant bien fort toi et Marcel
Moi Maurice j'écris quelques mots pour Marcel.

Je me trouve dans la même baraque que
ta sœur. Nous avons été rasés tous les enfants
de 4 à 18 ans. Je t'embrasse bien fort moi aussi
Un bonjour pour Mme [illegible], Mme [illegible] et
Mme Richard la crémière.
Marcel je te prie de bien vouloir dire à Mme Merle
que je lui est envoyer une lettre aussi pour un
colis. Et si elle reçoit pas ma lettre qu'elle me
l'envoyer à la même adresse que Annette.

Maurice [illegible]
Annette Gleizer
Destination
Annette Gleizer M. 34.
Baraque N. [illegible] Camp N°. 3.
Pithiviers
Loiret

Annette est toujours dans la même baraque

Chapter Nine

Drancy

Like Annette Gleiser, beginning on August 11, 1942, the children from Pithiviers and Beaune-la-Rolande were transported by train and in cattle cars to the internment camp in Drancy.

Many years later, in 1961, Dr. Georges Wellers was the only deportee from France asked to testify in Israel at Adolph Eichmann's trial in Jerusalem, as an eyewitness to the children's arrival. Dr. Wellers' recollections are particularly important because he was assigned as the doctor of Drancy camp for two and a half years. He was deported to Auschwitz and survived the death march to Buchenwald, which was liberated in April 1945 by the American army.

Eichmann coordinated deportations of Jews from Germany and elsewhere in western, southern and northern Europe to extermination camps. For this, he was indicted of crimes against humanity. For those, and other charges, he was sentenced to death by hanging and was executed on June 1, 1962. The execution of Adolph Eichmann is the only time that Israel has enacted a death sentence. From Dr. Wellers' testimony:

> In the second half of August 1942, four thousand children ranging in age from two to fifteen years were brought to Drancy without their parents, who already had deported to the death camps...These bewildered children...as they were unloaded into the yard from the buses that brought them, looked like a flock of little birds.
>
> Uniformed police guarded the buses and the surrounding barbed wire. As soon as the children left the buses they were directed to a room in a building. The older ones took the younger ones by the hand and held on during the climb to their rooms. Going up the stairs, the bigger children, out of breath, carried the little ones in their arms.

> Most of the children no longer knew where their belongings were. The few that had carried their packs seemed hindered by them. They stood in the room, frightened, huddled together, and hesitating for a long time before they would decide to sit on filthy mattresses on the floor.
>
> Meanwhile, the little bundles that had been left behind on the bus, were piled up in the yard. The children were told to fetch their belongings. The bundles without nametags were difficult to identify. Children four, five, and six years old walked around the piles trying to find their own bundles. After picking one up, they quickly looked inside surprised and perplexed to find a little dress or pants that did not belong to them.
>
> They would start searching again. There was no contention of any sort among them. To the contrary, they would try to help each other. After many unsuccessful attempts they would give up, standing, not knowing what to do next.
>
> Those wanting to return to their rooms would realize they did not remember where they were. They would politely beg in a soft voice to the adults supervising the operation, "I do not know where my little sister is. Maybe she is afraid to be by herself." Someone would lead the bigger ones by the hand or carry smaller ones in their arms going from floor to floor and room to room until the brother or sister was located. Their reunion was indescribably tender.

But trying to get settled in Drancy was only the beginning of the children's trials. Having so recently come from warm homes and loving families, they suddenly found themselves in a strange and harsh world where they had to sleep on dirty mattresses, endure terrible overcrowding, and worry constantly about having something to eat. In fact, food was so scarce in Drancy that in order to alleviate starvation, the internees were given coupons, which gave them the right to receive packages from the outside.

Among those who tried to seize this small opportunity was twelve-year-old Jacques Finkelstein. His parents and older sister and brother had been deported during the summer of 1942, and he was arrested in October along with his younger brothers Leon, 11 and Henri, 6, and their sister, Marcelle, 10. There is no record of where or how the children lived between the time of their parents' deportation and their own arrest. There is, however, a letter that Finkelstein wrote to a potential sponsor in hope of securing some additional food for his three younger siblings.

George Horan's eyewitness sketch of Jewish children arriving in cattle cars at Drancy.
(Photo: C.D.J.C.)

It is, in any case, unlikely that the Finkelstein children ever received any relief from their hunger. They were deported on convoy No. 40, which left Drancy on November 4 with a thousand Jews on board. They were among two hundred children deported in this convoy. They arrived at Auschwitz on November 6. Upon arrival, 269 men and 92 women were selected for work and tattooed with numbers on their forearms. The remaining 639 people, including the Finkelstein children, were sent immediately to the gas chambers. (S. Klarsfeld, *Le Memorial des Juifs de France*)

Several weeks before Jacques Finkelstein wrote this letter, on the night of September 23 my father learned through Resistance channels that the French police were going to start rounding up Jews of Romanian origin the next day. My mother's sister and her husband, Perla and Avram Cogan, were from Romania. So at seven thirty in the morning of the 24th, as Paris was waking up, I left our hiding place in the beauty salon and ran the miles to their place to warn them.

But when I arrived, their concierge said, "They were taken away ten minutes ago." I was too late! For years I lived with the thought that I had not run fast enough and that perhaps, had I been faster, I might have saved them. But I also wonder too, that had I been there earlier, I might have been arrested along with them.

Internees at the Drancy concentration camp. (C.D.J.C.)

A Letter from Drancy

For a brief time, Jews in Drancy were allowed to receive packages from sponsors outside the camp. In translation, this letter, written by a child seeking a sponsor, reads:

Drancy 31 October 1942

Dear Sir,

It is a poor Jewish child that writes to you. My name is Finkelstein Jacques, I am 12 years old. I am at this time interned in Drancy. I am in charge of the care of three young children who are my brothers and sister: Leon, 11; Marcelle, 10; and Henri, 6 years old. Our parents, Polish Jews, were deported three months ago as well as my big brother and my big sister. There is no one I know to send the slips which allow us to receive packages. It is to you that I entrust my last hopes.

I beg you, do something for my little brothers and sister. It breaks my heart to be unable to give them the bread which they ask me for which I do not have. I deprive myself daily for them, but it is not sufficient, because I have no other food. I miss everything, bread, chocolate, everything. I used to live in Ste Menehould, in the Marne. I have no other relatives left. I thank you in advance for the little ones and I believe with all my heart in your generosity.

Jacques Finkelstein

P.S.: I include in the envelopes of the little ones their slips for a package.

(Letter written by Jacques Finkelstein, 12 years old,
Drancy, bloc I, stairway 2, room 8)
DLXXXV, 2d, C.D.J.C.

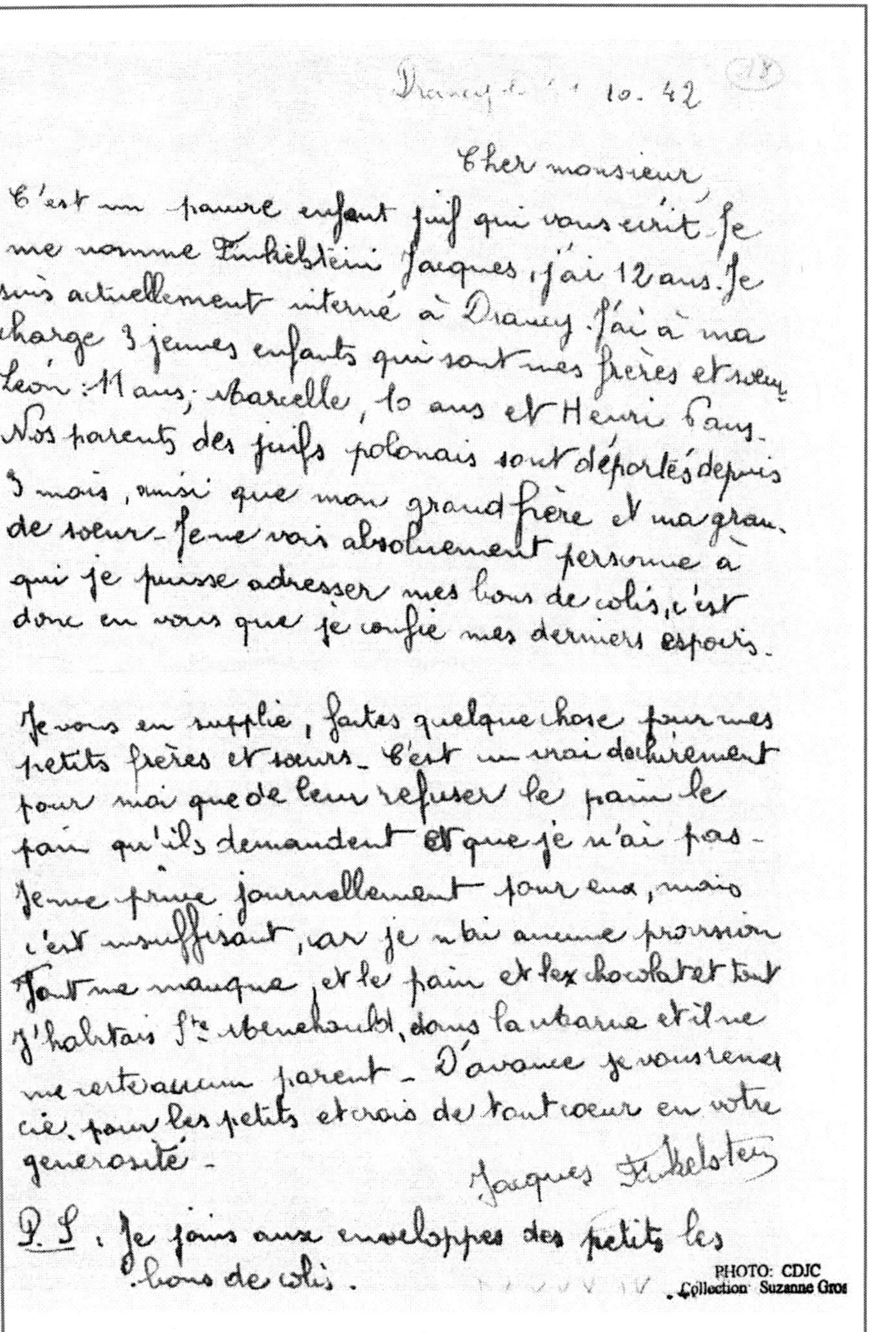

Drancy le [illegible] 10. 42 (28)

Cher monsieur,

C'est un pauvre enfant juif qui vous écrit. Je me nomme Finkelstein Jacques, j'ai 12 ans. Je suis actuellement interné à Drancy. J'ai à ma charge 3 jeunes enfants qui sont mes frères et soeur. Léon : 11 ans, Marcelle, 10 ans et Henri 6 ans. Nos parents des juifs polonais sont déportés depuis 3 mois, ainsi que mon grand frère et ma grande soeur. Je ne vois absolument personne à qui je puisse adresser mes bons de colis, c'est donc en vous que je confie mes derniers espoirs.

Je vous en supplie, faites quelque chose pour mes petits frères et soeurs. C'est un vrai déchirement pour moi que de leur refuser le pain le pain qu'ils demandent et que je n'ai pas. Je me prive journellement pour eux, mais c'est insuffisant, car je n'ai aucune provision. Tout me manque, et le pain et le chocolat et tout. J'habitais Ste Menehould, dans la Marne et il ne me reste aucun parent. D'avance je vous remercie pour les petits et crois de tout coeur en votre générosité.

Jacques Finkelstein

P.S. Je joins aux enveloppes des petits les bons de colis.

PHOTO: CDJC
Collection Suzanne Gros

My parents and I find ourselves in this place where we were given permission to write a few words before our departure.

I have nothing of interest to write about, but We hope to see you all again some day.

Excuse my handwriting, I am not writing in A good spot.

Your father and mother-in-law and Volf

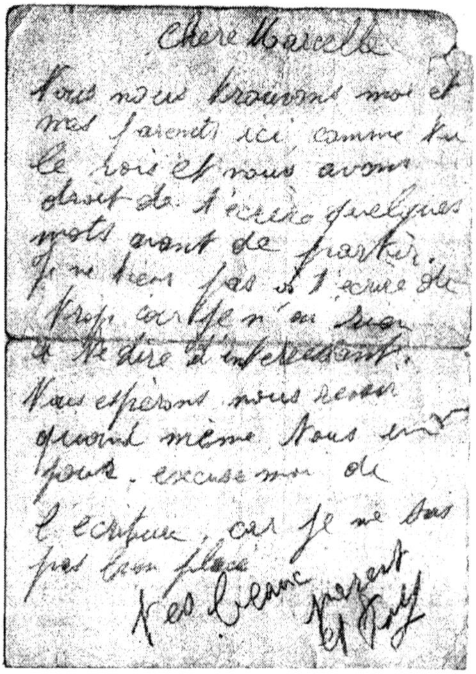

Chère Marcelle
Nous nous trouvons moi et
mes parents ici comme tu
le vois et nous avons
droit de t'écrire quelques
mots avant de partir.
Je ne tiens pas à t'écrire de
trop car je n'ai rien
à te dire d'intéressant.
Nous espérons nous revoir
quand même tous un
jour. excuse moi de
l'écriture, car je ne suis
pas bien placé
Nos beaux parents et Volf

Goodbye postcard from my cousin, Volf Cogan. (C.D.J.C.) After their arrest, Aunt Perla, Uncle Avram, and their son Volf were sent to camp Drancy, which was the transit camp, last stop before deportation to the death camps in the East. Volf, shortly before their deportation, was allowed to write a postcard to his brother Georges' wife, Marcelle. Although he did not know where they were being sent, he clearly wanted to communicate with his family as best he could.

Chapter Ten

French Trains to Auschwitz

A train arriving at Auschwitz. The letters SNCF on the train stand for *Societe Nationale de Chemins de Fer Francais* (French National Railways Society), and indicates that this was a French deportation train. (Photo: C.D.J.C.)

The first camp built by the Nazis in Auschwitz (Poland) was used simply to house a company of the German army's construction troops. But in the summer of 1941 its commandant, Rudolph Hess, was told by his superior that Adolph Hitler had given the order for the "Final Solution" of the Jewish question, and that Auschwitz had been chosen as one of the places in which that solution would be carried out. Auschwitz was selected for three reasons—it was accessible by rail, it was relatively isolated from populated areas, and its location made it possible to be concealed and its installations camouflaged.

By the following summer, Auschwitz, as well as other camps such as Buchenwald, Majdanek, and Sobibor, were in operation and ready not only for adults, but also for the children who had been incarcerated in the French camps of Pithiviers, Beaune-la-Rolande and Drancy. In fact by early August, the Vichy Interior Ministry and the French General Commissioner of Jewish Affairs had already worked out a schedule for the trains that would take these Jews to the "East."(Archival memorandum of August 3, 1942, pgs. 60-61.)

FRENCH STATE

Paris, August 3, 1942

THE PREFECT
of THE MINISTRY of the INTERIOR

TO Mr. GENERAL COMMISSIONER for
Jewish Affairs. Paris

Thank you for your letter of July 31, which gives me the planned train schedule for the deportation of foreign Jews towards the eastern territories.

Through the German authorities I was already acquainted with the details enclosed in your letter, and accordingly, I took the following actions so that the departures take place at the dates indicated herewith.

The trains of July 31, August 3, 5, and 7 consisted of foreign Jews arrested in Paris who had been transferred to the camps of Pithiviers and Beaune-la-Rolande. (Among them the mothers and fathers of four thousand children.) The trains of August 10, 12, and 17 will be composed of foreign Jews from the Free Zone. The trains will be going to the camp at Drancy where they will be taken over by the German authorities.

The trains of August 19, 21, and 24, and 26 will be mostly of children whose families had been interned in the camps of Pithiviers and Beaune-la-Rolande.

As for the trains of August 28 and 31, I have asked the Vichy Ministry of the Interior to have them made of Jews arrested or interned in the Free Zone. By that time all the Jews arrested in the occupied zone with their families will already have been deported.

Memorandum from Jean Leguay (French Police Representative of Jean Bousquet, head of the Vichy National Police) to Darquier de Pellepoix, General Commissioner for Jewish Affairs, regarding the scheduling of trains taking Jews from France to Auschwitz.

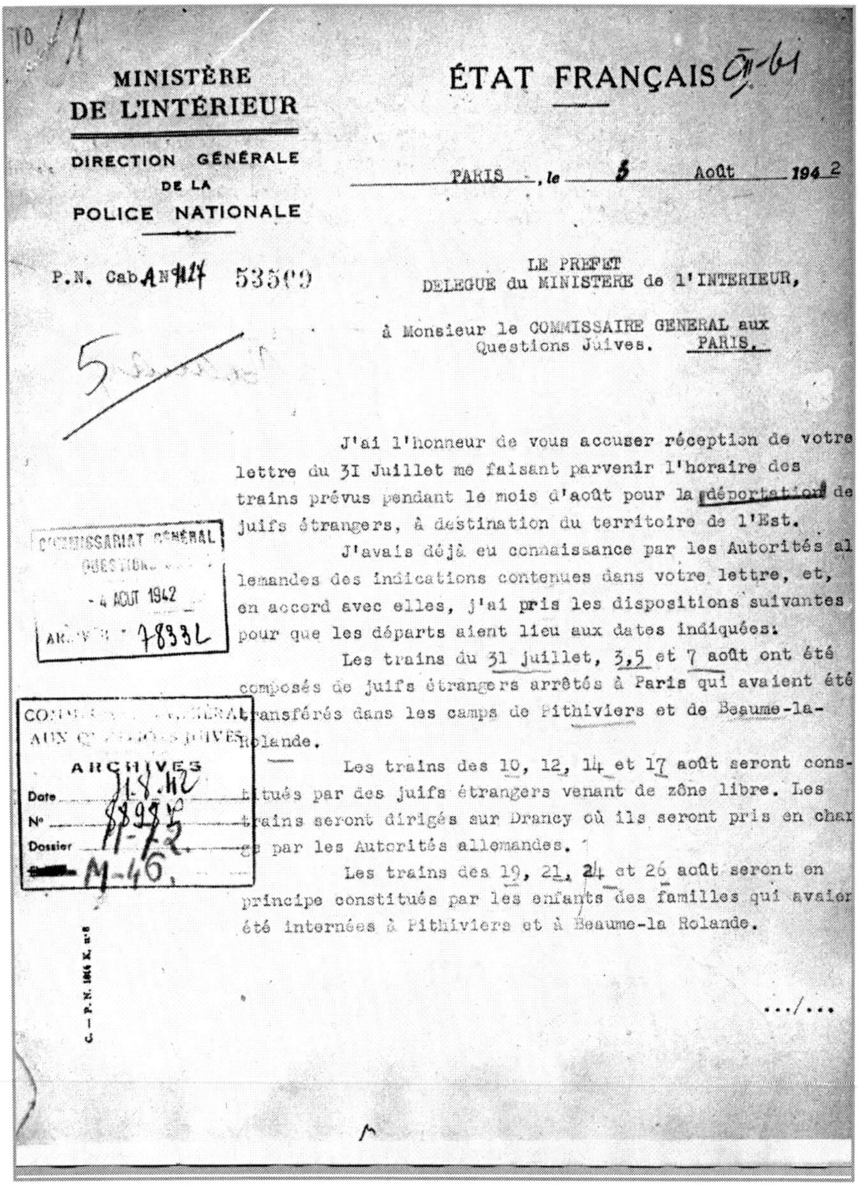

MINISTÈRE
DE L'INTÉRIEUR

DIRECTION GÉNÉRALE
DE LA
POLICE NATIONALE

ÉTAT FRANÇAIS 91-61

PARIS, le 5 Août 1942

P.N. Cab AN 4114 53569

LE PREFET
DELEGUE du MINISTERE de l'INTERIEUR,

à Monsieur le COMMISSAIRE GENERAL aux
Questions Juives. PARIS.

J'ai l'honneur de vous accuser réception de votre lettre du 31 Juillet me faisant parvenir l'horaire des trains prévus pendant le mois d'août pour la déportation de juifs étrangers, à destination du territoire de l'Est.

J'avais déjà eu connaissance par les Autorités allemandes des indications contenues dans votre lettre, et, en accord avec elles, j'ai pris les dispositions suivantes pour que les départs aient lieu aux dates indiquées:

Les trains du 31 juillet, 3,5 et 7 août ont été composés de juifs étrangers arrêtés à Paris qui avaient été transférés dans les camps de Pithiviers et de Beaume-la-Rolande.

Les trains des 10, 12, 14 et 17 août seront constitués par des juifs étrangers venant de zône libre. Les trains seront dirigés sur Drancy où ils seront pris en charge par les Autorités allemandes.

Les trains des 19, 21, 24 et 26 août seront en principe constitués par les enfants des familles qui avaient été internées à Pithiviers et à Beaume-la Rolande.

.../...

COMMISSARIAT GÉNÉRAL
QUESTIONS ...
- 4 AOUT 1942
AR... 7833L

COMMISSARIAT GÉNÉRAL
AUX QUESTIONS JUIVES
ARCHIVES
Date 11.8.42
N° 8899
Dossier 11-72
M-46

G — P.N. 1816 N. n°8

As already noted, the men were deported first, then the women, and finally the children. But mindful of appearances, in order to make it look like the despairing children were being deported with adults or family, a telex from Berlin ordered that "no transports should be exclusively of children."
(Archival telex of August 13, 1942: secret-urgent. C.U.J.C.)

Further testimony by Dr. Georges Wellers at Eichmann's trial in Jerusalem recalled the preparations of the children for that trip. We know now that the children were very much alone, mostly without loved ones, no matter whether they were two years old or fifteen years old. (Translations from excerpts of Wellers' testimony from his book: *De Drancy a Auschwitz.*)

> "On the eve of their deportation, during the second half of August 1942, the Jewish children in Drancy concentration camp, like the grown-ups underwent a search of their possessions. Toddlers two-and three-years-old, along with other children, would be led to the camp barracks where searches of their small bundles were taking place.
>
> The inspectors of the PHI (Jewish Question Police) would thoroughly rifle the small packs, then dismiss the children with their bundles in disarray. Little girls had their earrings and other jewelry confiscated.
>
> Near the exit was a table manned by volunteers who helped the children to repack their bundles. One ten-year-old girl came out of the barracks with a bleeding ear. When she could not remove her earrings fast enough, they were torn off.
>
> The day of the deportation, the children would be awakened at 5:00 a.m. and dressed in semi-darkness. Often there was a chill in the morning air. Because they had been awakened suddenly in the dark, the youngest children would start to cry. Little by little the other children would join in. At times a room was filled with as many as a hundred children wailing, overtaken by uncontrollable panic and refusing to be dressed. Policemen would be called upon to carry the children screaming in terror down into the chilly yard for the roll call, which preceded their deportation.
>
> Then, standing and waiting for their names to be called, the older children would hold the littler ones by the hand and would not let go of them. From time to time some of the children too young or too confused to remember their name, often answered the roll call incorrectly. When this happened, they were indicated on the day's deportation list by a question mark. The quota per convoy to the death camps was to be no less than a thousand Jews, so the children with unknown names were added at the last minute to complete this quota as needed.

In this manner, over a two week period, four thousand children were deported without their parents from Drancy." "One is left to imagine," Dr. Wellers added, "the voyage of those lamentable convoys packed with little children, across all of Europe; imagine those who yet had survived the trip, descend from the trains amidst armed SS, shouting, while accompanied by enormous barking police dogs. The children's last walk to the gas chambers, and their awful sacrifice to feed inextinguishable hatred."

One of the young people who had been transported from Drancy to Auschwitz was my eighteen-year-old cousin, Volf Cogan. Rather than being sent immediately to the gas chambers, as many were, Volf was instead selected to the forced labor camp of Blechhammer/Auschwitz IV. More than a year later, he was still alive—a testament to his strong will and determination to survive. He managed to send a letter to his sister-in-law. A partial translation of one of his letter is on the following page.

COUSIN VOLF

...I would like you to send me more pictures of everyone. In a few days I will receive your parcel, I will then send you another letter, so you can continue to send me more things, such as garlic, onions, peppers, vinegar, a little oil, candies, and especially fatty foods.

...I also need toilet articles, some camping utensils such as plates, forks, a tin mess, knives, and a good haversack, if possible...send some warm underwear for the winter, long underpants, undershirts, rubber slacks, very thick woolen socks, a leather cap, with earmuffs to protect ones ears, legging; two pairs of gloves, one in wool, one in leather. You might want to look ahead of time for a very thick pair of corduroy slacks which you could have ready to send when I write for them; a thick pair of slippers to wear inside large rubber boots; some thread, needles, thimble, and a belt. I also would appreciate a few books.

Have Marcel and Bernard jot a few words in your next letter. Tell them how happy it would make me. Nothing more to say for now.

Greetings to all my friends, and kisses

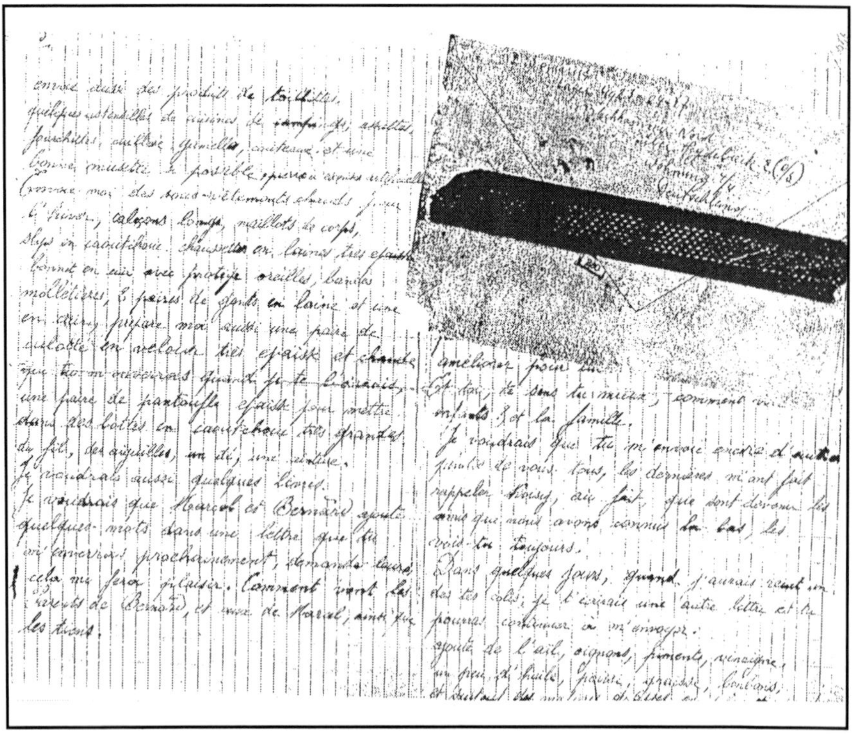
envoie aussi des produits de toilette,
quelques ustensiles de cuisine de campagne, assiettes,
fourchettes, une boîte gamelle, couteaux et une
bonne musette si possible
envoie moi des sous-vêtements chauds pour
l'hiver, caleçons longs, maillots de corps,
slips en caoutchouc, chaussettes en laine très épaisses
bonnet en cuir avec protège oreilles, bandes
molletières, 2 paires de gants en laine et une
en cuir, prépare moi aussi une paire de
culotte en velours très épaisse et chaude
que tu m'enverras quand je te l'écrirai,
une paire de pantoufles épaisse pour mettre
dans des bottes en caoutchouc très grandes
du fil, des aiguilles, un dé, une ceinture.
Je voudrais aussi quelques livres.
Je voudrais que Marcel et Bernard ajoutent
quelques mots dans une lettre que tu
m'enverras prochainement, demande leurs
cela me fera plaisir. Comment vont les

[redacted]

améliorer pour
Je voudrais que tu m'envoie encore d'autres
photos de vous tous, les dernières m'ont fait
Dans quelques jours, quand j'aurais reçu un
des tes colis, je t'écrirai une autre lettre et tu
pourras continuer à m'envoyer :
ajoute de l'ail, oignons, piments, vinaigre,
un peu d'huile, ...

Because Jewish prisoners were forbidden any contact with anyone outside the camp under penalty of death, Volf sent this letter under a borrowed name. The envelope (above), which with the letter is now in the possession of his sister-in-law, Marcelle Bernier Cogan, shows that the letter was opened by censors.

We never saw Volf again. In late January 1945, when the Soviet army was approaching Auschwitz to liberate the camp, the Nazis forced the remaining inmates on a death march to Gross Rosen, about 182 kilometers away. According to a survivor of the march, Volf may have either been shot while trying to escape or died on the march itself.

Chapter Eleven

In Hiding

Hiding in the boarded-up beauty parlor was very difficult for me. I would listen behind the cellar gate for steps on the tiled hallway or on the wooden steps of the stairways, and if I did not hear anything, I would run out…sometimes wearing the Star of David, sometimes not. Although I did not mean to, I was creating a safety problem for my parents, my sister, our devoted landlady, and Chaouche.

I told my mother that I did not belong inside, and once I had to stop going to school, that I did not belong outside either. My neighborhood friends played with me a bit, but they sensed that things were not like before. I could not invite them over. I could not go to the library with them, to the parks, or to the movies, because Jews were not permitted.

We were, of course, ignorant as to the final fate of the Jews who had been deported. We had no way of knowing that most of them would end up in the gas chambers and the crematoriums. Even if we heard rumors about it, we most likely would not have believed them. Who would have imagined that there were such things as "industrial killing" camps designed to reduce millions of people to ashes. As far as we knew, deportees were going to work camps in the "East," and because of this ignorance, we thought we could take a chance, go a distance to a soup kitchen of the U.G.I.F., or run out of our hiding places to get away from confinement, even if only for a little while. Eventually, though, my parents thought it would be best for all of us if they sent me to a U.G.I.F. children's home.

*****

The U.G.I.F. homes were created for children whose parents had been deported without them, or some of whose parents, like mine, were actually in hiding, or some whose were simply unable to sustain their care. So even though the U.G.I.F. functioned under the constraints of the Vichy government and the Gestapo, it was also able to serve as a front for such organizations as the O.S.E. *(Oeuvres de Secours des Enfants/Organization to Save the Children)* and *Le Dispensaire* (The Medical Clinic) in their efforts to safeguard Jewish children and young adolescents.

There were many U.G.I.F. homes, shelters, and orphanages for Jewish children in and around Paris, including rue Vauquelin, rue Lamark, rue des Rosiers, La Varenne St Hilaire, Louvenciennes, rue Guy Patin, St Mande, rue de Secretan, Neuilly sur Seine, Montreuil sous Bois, La Varenne and Montgeron.

Some of the children in the homes were also referred to as "blocked" children. They had been arrested with their parents but removed from overcrowded French concentration camps while awaiting deportation. They were, however, on a list of those to be deported, and later, when the quota of one thousand deportees per convoy could not be filled, the French police or the Gestapo would round up children from the U.G.I.F. homes to meet the required number of people.

In fact, late in the war, barely a month before the liberation, Alois Brunner, one of Eichmann's assistants ordered the arrest of all the U.G.I.F. children, whether blocked or not. Over three nights from July 20 to July 22, 1944 five hundred children were seized, and on July 31, three hundred children less than eighteen years old, some as young as two years old and one newborn with his mother, were among the thirteen hundred deportees taken in convoy No. 77 to Auschwitz. I was then in hiding with my mother in the beauty parlor.

I was first sent to La Varenne, which was a caring place. But when it was discovered that I had spots on my lungs, a possible sign of tuberculosis, I was switched to Montgeron, a so-called *Preventorium* for sick children. The "doctors" and "nurses" in Montgeron wore the traditional white medical garments (with the obligatory Star of David), but they didn't actually belong to the medical professions. They were simply Jews who, because they were employed by the U.G.I.F., were being safeguarded from arrest and deportation. But by the end of July 1943, like all other Jews, they would also be arrested and deported.

*****

UNION GENERALE DES ISRAELITES DE FRANCE

Montgeron, Paris, 15/1/1943

Preventorium - Centre 44, Dept. 17

Mr. General Secretary,

We are letting you know that today we have turned over to Madame Lazarus, social worker, eight children:

1 - Griffel Simone, "Rot hchild" orphanage

2 - Lotematejn Charles, " "

3 - Zaraya Daniel, 104 Boulevard Voltaire, Paris 11

4 - " Victor "

5 - " Sarah " "

6 - Daliez Michel, 12 Impasse Briard, Paris 9

7 - Szychter David, 25 Impasse Putigneux, Paris 4

8 - Pertzovsky Sarah, 109 rue des Haies, Paris 20

Sincerely yours. The

Director Mme. R.

Blousman

A letter from the director of the U.G.I.F. home in Montgeron to the General Secretary of the U.G.I.F. concerning the transfer of eight children, including my name, Sarah Perzovsky. (Collection: Yivo)

Because of my father's connections in the Underground, he heard months before that the children in the U.G.I.F. homes were under surveillance by both the French police and the Gestapo, and that there might be roundups in the future. So in order to protect me, my parents arranged that I be taken out of the home in Montgeron and returned to Paris to hide again with my mother and my sister.

I did not, however, stay long in Paris. Shortly after arriving there, I was sent with a guide, through an underground network to be hidden on a farm in the countryside. I would of course have loved to return to Courchamps to stay with the Demoncys, but I could not take refuge in a place where my identity was already known. En route, I slept in different

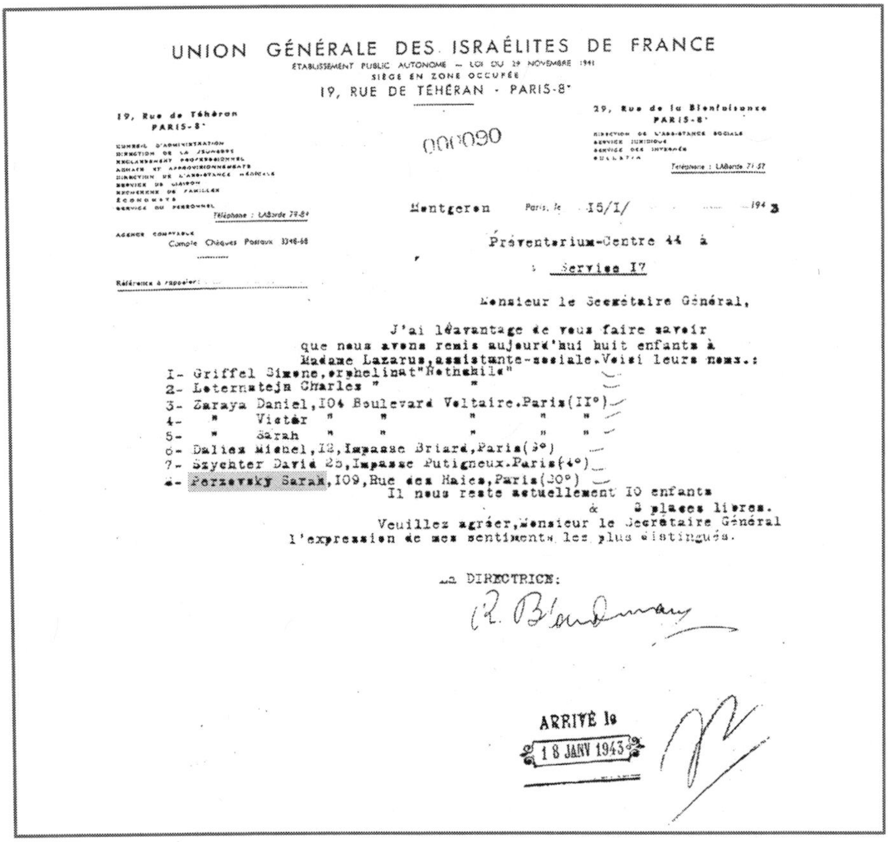

UNION GÉNÉRALE DES ISRAÉLITES DE FRANCE
ÉTABLISSEMENT PUBLIC AUTONOME — LOI DU 29 NOVEMBRE 1941
SIÈGE EN ZONE OCCUPÉE
19, RUE DE TÉHÉRAN - PARIS-8e

19, Rue de Téhéran
PARIS-8e

Téléphone : LABorde 79-84

Compte Chèques Postaux 3346-68

Référence à rappeler:

29, Rue de la Bienfaisance
PARIS-8e
Direction de l'Assistance Sociale
Service Juridique
Service des Internés
Téléphone : LABorde 71-57

000090

Montgeron Paris, le 15/I/ 1943

Préventorium-Centre 44 à
Service 17

Monsieur le Secrétaire Général,

J'ai l'avantage de vous faire savoir que nous avons remis aujourd'hui huit enfants à Madame Lazarus, assistante-sociale. Voici leurs noms.:

I- Griffel Simone, orphelinat "Rothschild"
2- Leternstejn Charles " "
3- Zaraya Daniel, 104 Boulevard Voltaire. Paris (II°)
4- " Victor " " " " "
5- " Sarah " " " " "
6- Daliez Michel, 12, Impasse Briard, Paris (3°)
7- Szychter David 25, Impasse Putigneux. Paris (4°)
8- Perzovsky Sarah, 109, Rue des Haies, Paris (20°)

Il nous reste actuellement 10 enfants
& 3 places libres.

Veuillez agréer, Monsieur le Secrétaire Général l'expression de mes sentiments les plus distingués.

La DIRECTRICE:
R. Blandurnay

ARRIVÉ le
18 JANV 1943

places as the four boys who joined the guide and I were picked up. During the train trip we were told not to wear the Star of David, and my name was completely changed from Sarah Pertzovsky to Suzanne Petro—another "me," which made me feel the separation from my parents and sister even more strongly.

After we had been traveling for a good while, the train came to a halt in the middle of the countryside. Suddenly there were men in civilian clothes and speaking German, running all over the train, obviously searching for someone. It was the Gestapo, and I thought for sure that they were looking for Jews! Our guide became agitated and quickly said to us, "We are not together. In case you are asked, you are going to visit family."

And then she left us! Standing at the window, I watched as the Gestapo ran by me. I was overtaken by fear, praying with all my soul that I would see my loved ones again. Finally, after what seemed a very long time, the train started to move again, slowly at first, and then faster. I was safe for the moment, but as I stood there I was overwhelmed by new feelings, by loneliness, and by fear of the uncertainty of the unknown away from my mother and father.

We were lined up—the four Jewish boys and me—in a dim room lit only by candles in someone's farmhouse. Several farmers were facing us, complete strangers, each of whom had come from the surrounding area to pick one of us to live and "hide" on their farm. It was embarrassing to be examined—goodness knows what they were looking for. I remember feeling overcome with sadness, and wishing that I could go with one of the boys so I would not feel so alone in this strange surrounding. Finally, a farmer woman pointed toward me and said, "I want her." I was making every effort not to cry.

To this day I do not remember the farmer woman's name, or her maid's name, but I recall that her son's name was Paulo. I am pretty sure the village itself was in Normandy, because of the typical interior: a large main room with a walk-in fireplace and alcoves on either side, each one with a double bed and a crucifix at the head above. Curtains could be drawn around the beds for privacy. There was the traditional big armoire filled with linens, a long table which seated quite a few people, and country chairs. There was also a magnificent bejeweled grandfather clock.

I was to sleep with the maid in a small room to the side of the main room. There was a stairway leading up to the attic where I was to store my belongings, which I left in a few piles on the floor. There was also a small window in the attic where I could gaze at the front yard and the sunset and where I would sit and cry. Life was so different! The first morning I was given a piece of broken mirror, which I secured against the stone wall outside in front of the house, I also was given a small rag and a little pot to fetch water from a brook a few yards away. This is the way I washed for five months.

I had many chores on the farm. I collected eggs, fed the chickens and rabbits, and helped to bring the cows back and forth from the fields. I would also weed, pick potatoes, and pull out the trunks of tall cabbages, working in the fields from morning till night. Many times, Paulo, who at ten, was half a year younger than I, would come with me. He was my only friend.

In the farmhouse I would clean, dust, sweep, and do the dishes. The maid did the cooking, the wash and took care of milking the cows and feeding them and the horses. I came to feel affection for the animals. I also loved the rich soil. But I felt no one cared about me. Only Paulo treated me like a human being.

Jewish children working at a farm where they were hidden in Southern France. Organizations such as Rue Amelot, Oeuvres de Secours des Enfants (O.S.E.) and the U.G.I.F. formed clandestine networks to save children and arranged for some to reside with non-Jewish families, who were paid (payments in YIVO archives) for the children's upkeep. (Photo: C.D.J.C.)

One day, as I was walking back from the fields, I saw a black car parked in front of the farmhouse and ran towards the wood as fast as my wooden shoes would allow me. I knew that only someone official would have a black car, so I stayed hidden in the woods for quite a while. When I got back, I was told that there were some inquiries about me and I would have to leave. I was so relieved! I would no longer be subjected to the whims of "the farmer lady." Ever since I had objected to working in the fields during heavy rains, I was deprived of Sundays' dessert, as punishment. The humiliation at the dinner table in front of the "others" was worse than the deprivation. I longed to kiss, hug and love again my mom! My sister! My dad! The only regret I had was leaving my little friend Paulo.

*****

But I wasn't on my way home. Instead, I was taken to another farm. It was most likely also in Normandy—I again recall the traditional interior—and I remember arriving there in a horse and buggy. This farm, though, was very humble. There was no electricity, and water was pulled from a nearby well. The lady of the house, Madame Marie, was a young woman in her twenties who was expecting a baby. Her husband worked as a hired hand on other farms, and would only come by every so often. They lived on the farm in exchange for taking care of the garden, a cow, a pig, chickens, geese, and rabbits. The owners were a city couple that came on occasional weekends and on vacation.

I felt needed at Madame Marie's and helped her as much as I could. Our main staples were the mushrooms we picked in the woods and some kind of frizzled white skin that Madame Marie brought home from the *charcuterie* once a week. I had never seen such food before! I was taught to recognize various species of mushrooms—those suitable for human consumption and those that were poisonous. It was quite interesting, at least until I grew tired of Madame Marie's mushroom recipe, which was a "white sauce" *(sauce blanche)* that was a pasty glue-like mixture of water and flour. Fortunately, on Sundays we would walk about half an hour through the woods to visit Madame Marie's parents and siblings and I could always look forward to having a regular meal there.

Then came the night when the much-anticipated event occurred—Madame Marie went into labor. She woke me up and asked me to fetch her mother and grandmother and I ran all the way through the woods, pursued by frightening and menacing shadows. Her mother and grandmother, in turn, sent someone to the village grocery store/café where one could call the doctor on the only telephone available in these surroundings. By the time the doctor and his wife arrived, there were already several women from the area waiting in the main room. I was very anxious, as I could hear Madame Marie straining under her labor pains. I learned, then, that giving birth to a baby must be quite painful.

But in the morning there was a beautiful baby girl, and every morning afterward I felt such joy when I ran to see the baby in her crib.

One day Madame Marie needed something from the grocery/café of the small village, and sent me to get it for her. While I was in the store, the mayor of the village, a reputed Nazi collaborator who happened to be there, became curious about me. By then, of course, I had learned to say as little as possible and just observe. For some reason, which I do not recall, he decided to quiz me about the capital of various countries. He asked me first about France's capital, which of course was Paris, which made me think that he was either trying to make fun of me or trying to trip me up. So when he asked me about the capital of England, because I remembered that listening to London's BBC was forbidden, I pretended not to know. Even so, this incident led to questions about who I was and made it necessary for me to be on the move again a few days later.

*****

From Madame Marie's farm I was taken on a few days trip by horse and carriage to a convent. By that time I was about twelve years old. I was instructed by the guide that I would have to hide my Jewish identity. My insides ached when I realized that I would be staying at a convent and that I would have to pretend to be what I was not. "Sarah" was overwhelmed. I wished that I could instead be in hiding with my mother and my sister, Charlotte, but I was not given the choice.

The process of adapting to convent life—to the church and its practices and to the convent school—made demands on me that were very hard to meet. I learned the prayers quickly because we prayed often, but I was frightened and humiliated when one of the sisters first asked me catechism questions. Because of my ignorance and, I think, my tears, she soon stopped calling on me.

My first encounter with Catholic doctrine, such as the Immaculate Conception of the Virgin Mary with Baby Jesus, left me perplexed. After all, I understood how Madame Marie's little baby girl had been conceived and assumed that Jesus would have been conceived the same way. I was also confused because my father had told me that Jesus was Jewish. I guessed, then, that Jesus and I were alike, both of us pretending to be Catholic. At least I wasn't alone. There was also one other thing I could feel positive about—the canticles we sang in church. I'd always loved music, and especially liked a particular "Kyrie."

The scariest experience was my first confession. There was so much I had to hide! Most of all that I was Jewish and that my name was Sarah Pertzovsky. It occurred to me that the secret of my identity might even be a mortal sin! What a liar I had become! I never thought I would have to lie because I was Jewish! After all, there was nothing wrong with being Jewish! I knew, though, that I had to confess to the right kind of sins so I would be believable. How I wished my little Parisian friend Suzette, who was Catholic, could have been there to help me. As I searched for answers in preparation for my first confession, I leafed through the catechism. Among the last pages, I found a list of sins, and picked a couple of them. I must have confessed to the right kind, because my confession did not give away my true identity. But I never accepted having to lie.

Chapter Twelve

Children

Hedwig Plaut

Those of us who survived did so in several different ways. Some, like me, were hidden, or miraculously survived life in the camps and some escaped to other countries. My friend Hedwig Plaut, who was born in Germany and came to France in 1938, was one of this last group.

Born in 1935, Hedwig came to Paris at the age of three and a half, sent by her single mother who could not care for her at the time. There she joined her grandfather, Adolph Plaut, who had taken refuge in France in 1933. Once there, like he and other Germans, she became "stateless." As she remembers it many years later:

> "My grandfather, 'Opa' as I called him, lived [on the] *rue de Charonne*, in one room.
>
> It was in the eleventh quarter of Paris, heavily crowded with Jewish immigrants. It was our oasis before it became our trap.
>
> The courtyards and the streets became the familiar world where Opa would take me along while he would sing to collect

(l) Hedwig Plaut, about 1941, and (r) 5 years old in 1943. (Coll. Hedwige Delcampe)

money for our subsistence. Windows would open and coins would be tossed to us.

My grandfather taught me dignity in life. His French with German intonation could bring doom upon us. His example developed within me discerning instincts. Opa was my unknown father...the mother that I had lost...my nonexistent brothers and sisters...my family. How he must have loved me! His memory has warmed my heart over this past half century.

Rue Amelot, a clandestine organization that helped the Jewish community and rescued children assisted Opa in placing me at the orphanage of La Varenne St Hilaire.

I remember waiting all week for Opa's visit on Sundays. Then came the time when I no longer saw him. He was deported in convoy No. 55, on June 23, 1943, to Auschwitz. He had been all I had left."

But between her grandfather's arrest and deportation, on February 10, 1943, the French police rounded up the children at the orphanage. As Hedwig remembered:

"Daylight had arisen, as I lay on my bed in the immense dormitory. The air was frozen.

I had been sleeping under a heap of blankets when I started to lie ever so flat while immobilizing my breathing and movements. How was I able to breathe? For I was breathing and no one saw me. My bed was flat...looked empty...I no longer existed. I heard a stampede on the stairways, shouts and yells in French, all was going on nearby, above and below. To not move...to breath with no motion...my heart was thumping so loudly in my temples.

A crash was heard as the door of the dormitory burst open...a wild race down my aisle...commotion as my friends are screaming with fear. Some men's low voices in French... more bursts...little by little the tumult was fading away...I must not move...I am not here. How long did I stay this way? There is a blank.

Hedwidge Plaut's escape to Switzerland, August/September 1943.

> I finally left my bed. The dormitory was empty. My friends? I cried. I have no recollection as to what followed that event. My whole life, I will never know. Where did I go? Where was I sent? During the following hours, what did I do? What did I hear? I cannot say.
>
> Although frozen with fear, all the details should have imprinted in my memory forever.
>
> Will the tongue one day, suddenly, utter the monstrous event which forever penetrated my mind and body? The pull of terrifying forces that fell upon me...to escape...fear had saved me."

Left behind in the orphanage, Hedwig was subsequently taken in Paris, then in Michelet.

But Hedwig was returned to Paris in the summer of 1943 to join a group of children being smuggled across the border to Switzerland. The trip was filled with perils. The children had to be prepared and the many stages of the trip had to be explained to them. It would require an exchange of relayed guides at different places. There might be encounters with German patrols. The walking would take place mostly during the night, in silence and in the snow. Some of the other groups trying to escape had been caught, arrested, and deported. As she remembered:

> "The journey was dramatic and endless. Some children were lost on the way. Out of twenty-nine, only fourteen made it to Switzerland. We were told to keep going...not to look back...at times to run and hide. We reached the barbed wires of the border into Switzerland on September 14, 1943.
>
> To whom do I owe this escape? To this day, after many years of research and long lapses of memory, I still do not know."

ARRONDISSEMENT TERRITORIAL

N 13121

Genève, le 17-9-43.

24. SEP. 1943

S T A T E M E N T

Concerning

P L A U T : Edwige, bomon?, 1935, in Paris is too young to give her identification. French, Jewish, last address/Mme Nicolas, 177 route de Choisy a Ivry (Seine).

She states: I have not seen my parents since the age of three. They were deported and I no longer heard from them. I went to be with my Grandfather, who was also deported. I was then put in an orphanage in Paris, then at another lady's place, still in Paris, then somewhere else in Michelet. A young man came to take me back to Paris. From there, I was led with twenty nine other children by young people towards the boder.

We crossed the border September 14, around 11:30 near Comiere. As soon as we crossed, I was led to the custom's office, then to the police station and after to a reception center.

Sanitary inspection: Done and then taken to the hospital to be treated for scabies.

Means of subsistence:none

Training: none

Identity Papers: none

Flüchtlingskartothek
E.: 25.Sep 1943
Erledigt:

Lu et confirmé :

Plaut Edwige

(Hedwige Plaut Delcampe collection)

ARRONDISSEMENT TERRITORIAL

N 13121

Genève, le 17-9-43.

24. SEP. 1943

D E C L A R A T I O N

Concernant :

P L A U T Edwige, née le ? ? 1935 à Paris, n'est pas en âge de donner son état civil. Française, juive. dernier dom. c/ Mme. Nicolas, 177 bis route de Choisy à Ivry (Seine),

Elle déclare : Je n'ai pas revu mes parents depuis l'âge de trois ans. Mes parents ont été déportés et depuis je n'ai plus eu de nouvelles d'eux. Je suis ensuite allé chez mon grand-père, puis il a été déporté aussi. Puis j'ai été mise dans une colonie d'enfant à la Varenne, puis j'ai été dans un horphelina à Paris, puis j'ai été chez une dame à Paris et une autre à Michellet. C'est un jeune garçon qui est venu me chercher à Michelet et m'a conduit à Paris. De là j'ai été conduite avec 29 enfants et nous étions accompagnés par des jeunes gens du côté de la frontière.

Nous avons passé la frontière le 14-9-43 vers les 2330 dans la région Cornière. Dès notre passage j'ai été conduite au poste de douane puis au poste de gendarmerie et ensuite au centre d'acceuil des cropettes.

Visite sanitaire : effectuée et conduite à l'hôpital pour traiter la galle.

Moyens d'existence : aucun

Connaissances : aucune

Pièces d'identité : aucune

Flüchtlingskartothek
E.: 25. Sep. 1943
Erledigt:

i/f. G.A. Geiger

Lu et confirmé :

Plaut Edwige

Collection: Hedwige Delcampe

Danielle and Nicole Boruchowicz and their older sister, Simone

Simone Burochowicz was fifteen years old when the traumatic experience of separation from her loved ones occurred. The second of five children, she first saw her father taken away, then her mother, and was eventually separated from her brothers and sisters. They had been, as she remembered, "a happy family."

> Five children, Papa and Maman, such was our family at the dawn of deportations and tears. Papa was a tailor who worked long hours into the night with Maman's help on occasions.
>
> Then, came the terrible day of August 20th. Sounds of boots resounded up and down the stairways. There were knocks on nearby doors, and everywhere. We kept quiet, each one of us with our own fear except for our five-and-a-half month [old] twin girls. What did we have to fear? After all, we were a family with many children, honest, never in trouble. Why would we be arrested? Maman went out food shopping around eleven-thirty.
>
> As twelve o'clock came around, there was a knock on the door. They came in, two of them, knocking everything around, searching everywhere. The policemen gave furtive glances towards our sleeping little sisters...then they got hold of Papa. I ran down past a policeman on watch at the front door on the street...found Maman at the grocery store. I did not have to say anything—she understood. As we arrived, Papa was at the bottom of the stairway, surrounded by two policemen; my big sister and my little brother nearby were watching. It was so sudden! So unbearable for Maman. Frantic, she stood in Papa's way as he was trying his utmost to control himself. My mother's words of sorrow and protest, as she was still holding in her hands our daily bread and milk, did not in the least disturb the sarcastic policemen.
>
> Thus our life started with a new emptiness—a letter every eight days, a package sent every two weeks, tears and longing. As my older sister went to work, my little brother and I continued our schooling.
>
> First deportations, first air alerts. Second deportation...Papa was among them. It was June 1942. The school year was over and vacation time was just around the corner. Maman seemed happy to still have us around her. New anti-Jewish laws came about: no more park for our little babies, no public swimming pool, no

movies. Then another gigantic awful roundup took away mothers, children, and entire families. We were fearful as to what was to come. Our little twin sisters, Danielle and Nicole, had become fearful enough to run and take refuge in our arms, if they heard loud steps in the stairway...only sixteen months old, and they seemed to sense the danger.

October, on the eve of the first day of school, Maman had to renew some identity papers. She left taking the babies with her. We were preparing our school things. Then came 6:30 p.m. and Maman was not back. Our big sister came home from work. She ran to the police headquarters. It was closed. The policemen on watch had no information.

Eight o'clock, a knock! Maman is there with the twins followed by two docile German Shepherds and a decorated policeman. Small packs were put together for Maman, and then came the *adieux*.

The silence and the darkness of night arrived. It was cold. Oh, my little sisters how they cried. They knew in the darkness, that it was not Maman looking over them. In the night I was pleading, "But they did no harm!" The next day we went to say more goodbyes to Maman at the police station. The following month, we received three letters and sent a package. Then, no news at all. Deportation for Maman to an "unknown destination." Nothing has been heard from our parents in the past three years.

The five of us stayed together after those terrible events. One month later, we received summons. My two little baby sisters were taken to a U.G.I.F. nursery. My brother, Armand and myself were taken to the center, Guy Patin, also a U.G.I.F. children's home controlled by the French police and the Gestapo.

Another atrocious round up came on February 11, 1943, when tiny little children and bigger ones, silently, without one cry, holding their little packs, walked towards buses. The policemen coldly slammed the doors shut.

Around mid-February, upon warnings of another impending round up of children, twenty-five non-Jewish women, members of MNCR (National Movement Against Racism), with the help of Pastor Vergueras, pretended to take sixty-three children on an outing. Instead they placed them in safe houses or with Christian families willing to keep the children in hiding. Simone and Armand were saved along with those children. Their twin sisters also survived. Their parents perished.

Today, in her small apartment in Paris, Nicole likes to host, the friends who were raised with her in the home of the *Renouveau* (Renewal). Right after the war, this particular group, orphaned by the Holocaust, was placed at the *Renouveau* under the care of pedagogues. They guided and emphasized the children's education to make up schooling they had missed, but also to achieve, depending on their individual interest and capacity. To this day, as I had had the privilege to be invited to their gatherings as adults, they are like a family and care a great deal about one another. But all are deeply affected by the trauma of separation and loss of their parents.

Nicole and Danielle Boruchowitz at age two years and four months, photographed at the U.G.I.F. nursery of Neuilly on July 3rd, 1943.
(Photo: Nicole Fain and Danielle Boruchowitz collection.)

Chapter Thirteen

Stories Never Told

Although Hedwige Plaut and Simone Boruchowicz lost their families, they lived to tell their trials. But there are so many more that did not, so many whose stories will never be told. The individual dehumanization that they suffered until they met their final fate is buried in the cruelty of the Holocaust.

There were almost five thousand children who were still interned in Drancy as late as April 1944. Only a few months before France was liberated by the Allies, these children were sent to Auschwitz. There were also the children from the U.G.I.F. homes in Louvenciennes, near Versailles. After the war their caretaker, Denise Holstein, recalled how she and the children where taken from the home, their harrowing journey by freight train, and their eventual arrival at Auschwitz. She remembered how, on arrival, she was cautioned by inmates not to carry or lead a child by the hand during selection, because doing so would mean being immediately selected for death. Later she witnessed adults carrying or leading children, as well as other children and the elderly being directed toward trucks that took them to the gas chambers. All her charges were murdered. She was the only survivor.

[illegible]p de Drancy
[illegible]ureau de Commandement

Le 1[illegible] Avril 1944

NOTE pour l' U.G.I.E.

En réponse à votre note du 9 ct., nous avons l'honneur de vous communiquer les renseignements suivants :

I°) Nombre d'enfants de moins de 9 mois : 312

2°) Nombre d'enfants de 9 mois à 3 ans : 639

3°) Nombre d'enfants de 3 ans à 6 ans : 1053

4°) Nombre d'enfants de 6 ans à 13 ans : 2959

5°) Quantité de lait actuellement perçues pour tous ces enfants par mois : 2267,5 litres (Ces indications correspondent au mois de Mars 1944).

6°) Nombre d'enfants de moins de 9 mois absolument intolérants au lait frais et auxquels il faudrait donner une ration régulière de lait concentré; actuellement : -Deux-

7°) Nombre d'enfants de 9 mois à 3 ans ne pouvant pas digérer le lait frais; actuellement : -Deux-

En raison des "sautes" d'effectif très fréquentes, les renseignements que nous vous donnons, même basés sur un mois, ne peuvent donner qu'une idée approximative de la situation des enfants rationnaires en lait. Le nombre des enfants peut se trouver augmenté du jour au lendemain de 50 unités, le cas s'est produit il y a une huitaine.

Quant à la question du lait concentré, il est très difficile d'envisager ce problème sans tenir compte : D'une part des accidents (lait qui tourne); dans ces cas là, il est absolument indispensable de remplacer ce lait tourné par du lait concentré, (au moins pour les nourrissons et les enfants malades, nous ne parlons pas ici des vieillards qui ne se nourissent que de lait). D'autre part, il faut tenir compte des départs, ravitaillement du ou des wagons sanitaires, ravitaillement des enfants et des vieillards à qui les vivres doivent être assurés au départ pour un voyage de X jours; (à titre d'exemple, il a été donné pour les wagons sanitaires seulement : 100 boîtes de lait concentré).

Nous espérons que ces renseignements vous suffiront afin de vous permettre, de nous faire obtenir les rations de lait indispensables aux nourrissons et aux bébés qui ne passent hélas, ici, qu'en transit.

PHOTO: CDJC

Note to the U.G.I.F. from official at Drancy: Milk needed for babies and children.

"Milk is to be provided for the interned infants and babies who are unfortunately with us in a transit situation."

Camp of Drancy Headquaters April 18, 1944

NOTE for the U.G.I.F.

As a reply to your inquiry we forward to you the following information:

1) Number of children less than 9 months 312
2) Number of children 9 months to 3 years old 639
3) Number of children 3 years to 6 years old 1053
4) Number of children 6 years to 13 years old 2959
5) The quantity of milk needed for all the children is estimated to be monthly: 2267.5 liters. This is based on the needs in March 1944.
6) The number of children under 9 months who are unable to digest fresh milk and who are required regular rations of concentrated milk are 2.
7) The number of children 9 months to 3 years who cannot digest fresh milk now are 2.

Due to the frequent variation of the number of children in the camp, the information we give you at this time cannot accurately determine the actual needs in the future. The number of children can increase by 50 one day to the next, which is what happened 8 days ago.

As for concentrated milk, it is difficult to predict problems such as milk turning sour which needs to be replaced, at least for the infants, not counting the elderly people. On the other hand, we must consider the departures and*supplies which we must give to each freight car for a 10-days duration.

We hope the information we give you will help us get the milk rations necessary for the infants and babies who are unfortunately with us only in a transit situation.

*The U.G.I.F. was responsible for the food distribution to the deportee's convoys to the death camps.

Rothschild Hospital Maternity Ward in Paris, 1943. All were deported.(C.D.J.C.)

The children of the U.G.I.F. home of Louvenciennes with their caretaker. (C.D.J.C.)

The boys of the O.R.T. School, 4 rue des Rosiers, in the Jewish quarter of Paris. (C.D.J.C.)

Then, too, there were the babies from the maternity ward in the Rothschild Hospital in Paris who were sent with their mothers to Auschwitz in July 1943, the boys from the O.R.T. School on the *rue des Rosiers* in Paris, some of whose fate has never been determined, as well as the children from hundreds of other institutions and organizations all over France. But there were those who left messages that survived. One of them was Marcel Chetovy. Born in Paris on August 22, 1926, Marcel Chetovy was not yet eighteen years old when he was deported on July 31, 1944. But before he was taken away, he scribbled this message on the wall in Drancy that speaks volumes about the human spirit.

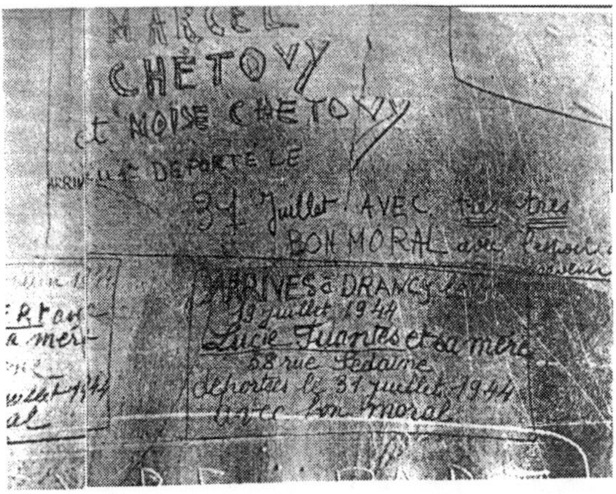

MARCEL CHETOVY and MOISE CHETOVY arrived on the 1st; deported the 31 of July in VERY GOOD SPIRITS with the hope of COMING BACK.

Another, whose heart-rending message has survived, is that of Liliane Gerstein. She was born on January 13, 1933, and was among forty-four children deported from the home of Izieu, near Lyon, under Gestapo chief Claus Barbie's order. Liliane wrote a letter to God a few days before she was deported on April 6, 1944, on convoy No.71 to Auschwitz, where she was put to death.

God? How good you are, how kind you are. If one were to count the good deeds and the many kindnesses you grant us, one would go on counting endlessly. God? You are the one who commands, you are justice itself.
You reward those who are good and you punish those who are mean. God? In the end, I can say I will never forget you. I will think of you always, even during the last moments of my life. You can be sure that, even if it is difficult for me to put it into words. How good you are. God? It is thanks to you that my life was beautiful before, that I was spoiled and had beautiful things that other people did not have. God? After all this I am asking you for one thing only:
MAKE MY PARENTS COME BACK, MY POOR PARENTS, PROTECT THEM (EVEN MORE THAN ME). MAKE IT POSSIBLE THAT I SHOULD SEE THEM SOON. MAKE THEM COME BACK SOON ONE MORE TIME.
Ah! I can say that I had such a good Mama and Papa. I have such faith in you, that I thank you ahead of time, right now.

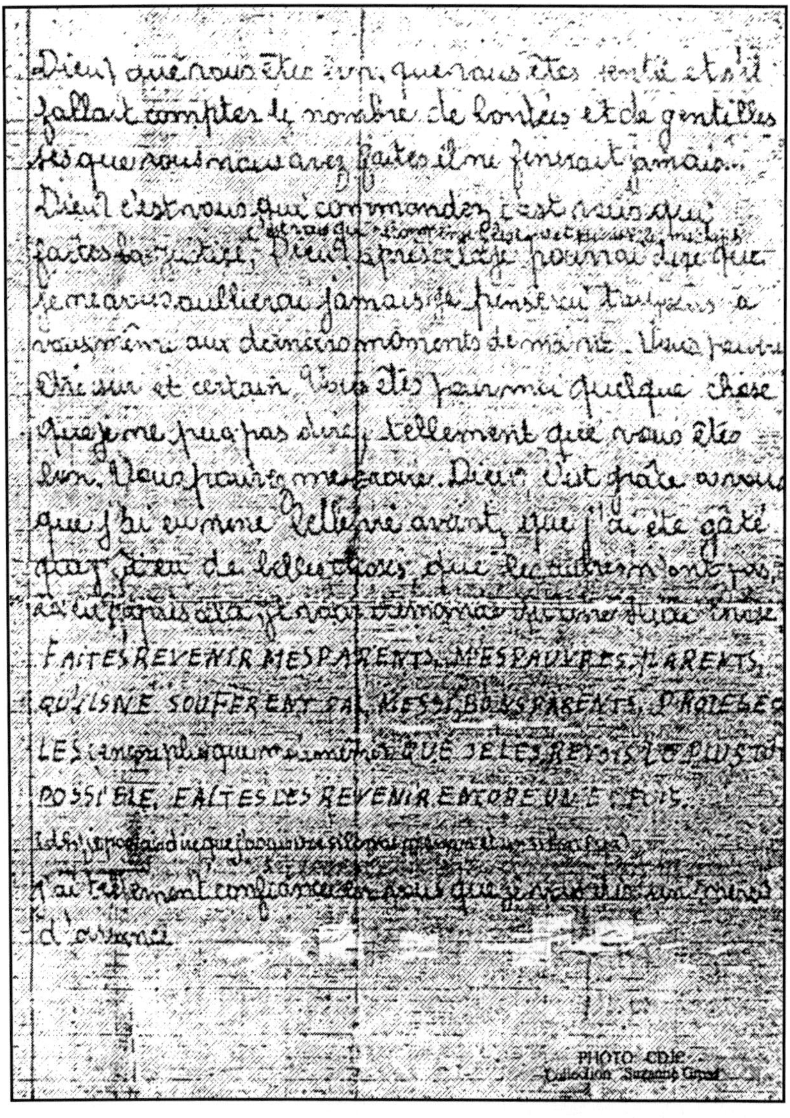

Dieu! que vous êtes bon, que vous êtes gentil et s'il fallait compter le nombre de bontés et de gentillesses que vous nous avez faites il ne finirait jamais...
Dieu! c'est vous qui commandez, c'est vous qui faites la justice, Dieu! à présent je pourrai dire que je ne vous oublierai jamais, je pense toujours à vous même aux derniers moments de ma vie. Vous pouvez être sûr et certain. Vous êtes pour moi quelque chose que je ne peux pas dire, tellement que vous êtes bon. Vous pouvez me croire. Dieu! C'est grâce à vous que j'ai eu une belle vie avant, que j'ai été gâtée, que j'ai eu de belles choses que les autres n'ont pas. [illegible]

FAITES REVENIR MES PARENTS, MES PAUVRES PARENTS, QU'ILS NE SOUFFRENT PAS, MES BONS PARENTS. PROTEGEZ LES (encore plus que moi-même) QUE JE LES REVOIS LE PLUS TOT POSSIBLE. FAITES LES REVENIR ENCORE UNE FOIS.

[illegible]

J'ai tellement confiance en vous que je vous dis merci d'avance.

PHOTO CDJC
Collection Suzanne Girad

CHAPTER FOURTEEN

The Winds of Freedom

After being hidden in the country for close to a year, in January 1944, I was brought back again to Paris to hide with my mother and sister. At home finally, in the boarded-up beauty parlor, I was able to promise my mom that I would no longer run out into the street. The ordeal of the separation from my loved ones while in the children's homes, on the farms, and in the convent, had tempered my childish, carefree nature. I was older—close to thirteen—and had come to understand our situation: We Jews, if caught for deportation could be sent to "unknown destinations." Although there was much we did not know, we knew that Jews were being sent away locked in railroad cars usually used to transport animals or various materials. We knew too, that even children, women, and elderly people were being sent to "work camps in the East." All this did not bode well.

To pass time quietly, my mother taught my sister and me how to knit and sew. Off and on, I re-read some of my favorite books, such as *La Mare au Diable (The Devil's Pond)* by George Sand, or *La Case de l'Oncle Tom (Uncle Tom's Cabin)* by Harriet Beecher Stowe. I also read the books my father brought me about my favored subject—history. But I missed the companionship of my friends. I missed my school terribly. I missed going out to play, to take walks, to roam around my neighborhood, to be out in the daylight, to feel the air on my face. I missed! I missed!

I would daydream about the future and reflect on the present. Why did this happen to Jews? I could not think of anyone of us who was dishonest or ill willed. My parents, their friends, my aunt and my uncle, our acquaintances...all worked diligently to make a living. There were good feelings among us. My sister and I felt such warmth and happiness. We got along with our neighbors, French or not. Why were Jews hunted? I heard the grownups talking about racism, Fascism, and anti-Semitism, but I didn't really understand what those words meant or how destructive those forces were.

I would also take long naps during the day and look forward to visits at night. Madame Blanchard, our devoted concierge, might come in with something to eat. Our friend Chaouche would show up with the latest news. My cousin Georges would drop by.

Having recovered from the agony of his internment in Drancy, he now was transporting arms for the Resistance. We hoped for the return of my dear aunt, uncle and cousin. My father, as a member of a Jewish partisan group, would also come in every so often with food. I would watch him move small pins on a European map on the wall to mark the advancing Russian army. We heard with wonder and pain about the long uprising of the Warsaw Ghetto. We were aware of the struggle during the battle of Stalingrad, but hopeful.

Meanwhile, my sister and I watched life on the street through the cracks in the shutters. Deprived of a normal life and aching to be free, we wondered when, who, and what would set us free.

*****

In August 1944, the winds of freedom arrived with the Allies approaching and the battle for the liberation of Paris first initiated by the French Resistance fighters—the F.F.I. (*Force Francaise de l'Interieur*) and the F.T.P. (*Franc-Tireurs et Partisans*). There was shooting on the rooftops between them and die-hard Nazi collaborators.

Back and forth, armed men with F.F.I. and F.T.P. armbands were scurrying by in open trucks. Policemen wearing these armbands, transformed into Resistance fighters, joined them, and Paris was freed on August 22, 1944.

Like everyone else, my mother, sister, and I finally came out in the street. We started to help build a barricade nearby in order to keep enemies—such as *Collabos* (collaborators) or German soldiers-from fleeing. And then, suddenly, a German tank appeared near the police station on the corner. Within a split second, the streets were deserted. We ran up to our apartment to watch through the slits of the closed shutters.

Several Resistance fighters were holed up in the back of the movie house across the street from the police station and one of the German soldiers shouted through a bullhorn that if they didn't come out the building would be stormed. I can still see the six men coming out, arms up, holding white cloths of surrender. The Germans hurriedly searched them one by one. And then, suddenly, two sharp, dry sounds pierced the air. Two Resistance fighters were shot at close range! In desperation, the men ran a few yards with bullets in their bodies, and then, finally, fell and lay in pools of their own blood. To our final anguish, with their untimely deaths, these two heroes perished even while the winds of freedom were blowing through the streets of Paris.

Memorial plaque for two French Resistance fighters.

"Those who are heartless, preach to us Forgiveness."
French poet and resistance fighter, Paul Eluard,
"Au Rendez vous Allemand" -- 1944.

Once the Germans were gone, the neighborhood came to life again; people near the barricade were talking with excitement, shaking hands, and kissing. There was happiness in the air! I felt the urge to again embrace the familiar streets of my neighborhood, those streets I'd been barred from for so long, and started to run through them. At last I was breathing the air outside, thrilled by the feel of the breeze on my face and the bright light of day! The war was over! The dark days of hiding were over! I was thirteen years old, and felt free again!

Chapter Fifteen (Epilogue)

To This Day

One day shortly after the liberation, a young American soldier knocked on our door and told us he was my first cousin, Joe Pertofsky. We were beside ourselves with joy! He was glorious and it was wonderful to feel the warmth of family again. My parents subsequently renewed contact with our American relatives—my father with his two older brothers in New York and a sister in Washington—and my mother with her two older brothers in Philadelphia.

While we had survived the Holocaust, my parents, wanting to leave those bitter memories behind them, no longer wished to live in France and applied for visas to immigrate to the United States. It was three years before the visas became available, but in 1948 they and I came to live in America. My sister Charlotte remained in Europe and married, but in 1957 she, her husband, and their three children also came to live here. I got married in 1951 and later had three children—two daughters and a son. After my father passed away in 1973 and my mother in 1983, I felt that their lives had reflected the wandering of Jews in the Diaspora.

In 1926, they left a life of poverty and struggles in Russia; they put their hope into France, which they also left in 1948, to live in the U.S. with little from the fruit of their work and after much suffering. But most of all they were alive, when so many Jews had perished during the Holocaust as throughout other periods of Jewish history.

Although we established a good life in America, I was always conscious of the losses we had suffered, and the differences between us and those who had not endured what we had. Even though, for example, I was welcomed wholeheartedly by my parents' American family, I was very aware of the fact that they had no idea of what this "Hidden Jewish Girl" had endured. And much as I tried, I could not love them like dear Aunt Perla, Uncle Avram and Volf, who had perished in the Holocaust. Was it an inability to abandon a profound and loving attachment? Was it fear of betrayal? Probably it was both.

For a long time, my parents, sister and I were haunted by the fact that we had no knowledge as to the final turmoils of our other dear family members. I often wondered what had happened to them on that fateful day in 1942? Where were they taken? How were they treated? Were they separated? They must have been so terrified! We knew that they were no longer alive, but there had been no funeral, and there was no grave we could visit. Nor had we mourned them according to our ancient Jewish customs.

That is, we did not sit *shiva*—stay at home for seven days following the funeral—so that family and friends could come to comfort and pray with us. We knew that their Jewish souls had been brutalized and torn, but the wounds of sudden and terrible loss had never been acknowledged.

It was only many years later that we finally learned what had happened to them. In 1978 Serge Klarsfeld, historian and activist, published his ground breaking *Memorial to the Jews deported from France*, which listed the names of the deportees according to the convoys in which they were included. In it we learned that convoy No. 37, which went to Auschwitz, was primarily made up of Roumanian Jews—473 men, 531 women, and 127 children less than seventeen years of age. Romania, being allied with Germany, had communicated through their embassy that "Romania was no longer interested in their Jews." And there on the list were the names of Perla and Avram Cogan and that of my dear cousin Volf. When I first saw their names on the page, I caressed them with my fingers.

*****

For many years I had not dwelt on the events of the Holocaust and particularly tried to shield my children from them. As a protective mother I decided not to talk to them about the Holocaust and instead to deal with the subject only when and if it arose. I wanted my children to be happy Americans. But as they were growing up, they saw family photographs, overheard conversations, and on occasion witnessed reactions. Whenever they asked questions, I would answer with the truth. One of those questions came one day from my nine-year-old son. After I answered, he looked at me with his wonderfully expressive eyes and said, "Psychologically it is not good for your children to tell them things like that." It was, however, important to me to share certain people from my past with my dear husband. On one of our trips to Paris, although I knew

Madame Blanchard had passed away, I also knew that I would find Chaouche at a certain time at his Algerian café. Our reunion was filled with emotion and affection and it brought all three of us much happiness.

Even though I have tried to look ahead rather than behind, there are times when memories spring up. One time I was waiting to cross a boulevard in Paris when a combination of the sound of German tourists and a sight of a bus filled me with memories of buses filled with Jews on their way to the concentration camps. On another trip, a more recent one, I went to my childhood neighborhood to take photographs and stopped in front of what used to be my kindergarten and elementary school. Much to my surprise, near the front door, I saw there was a recently placed plaque commemorating the Holocaust.

Reading the plaque made me realize something I had clearly erased from my memory—the fact that I must have had Jewish schoolmates who, after one or another roundup, had disappeared. Why didn't I remember that? Or were they deported when I was in hiding in the beauty parlor, or in one of the U.G.I.F. homes, on one of the farms, or in the convent? I don't know. The plaque also brought to mind the fact that this school had witnessed both the happiest days of my early school years—when I first began to appreciate the joy of learning—and the most difficult, when I had to wear the Star of David for the first time.

And finally, I felt now, at this time of my life, a gnawing chagrin to be yet in front of another plaque commemorating those who, unlike me, never lived out their childhood, never knew the excitement of adolescence, never grew to adulthood, never raised a family or had a career...and all of whom were innocent.

*****

I understand now that it is not possible to bury memories of the Holocaust. Nor do I have the right to forgive the suffering of my Aunt Perla, of my Uncle Avram, of my young cousin Volf, of his brother Georges, or of any of the other millions of victims of the Holocaust. I understand, too, that it is the fact of my survival and my moral strength that now makes it possible for me to confront the past and the catastrophic destruction of European Jewry during World War II known as the *Shoah*.

THE MEMORIAL PLAQUES AT MY SCHOOL

ARRESTED BY THE VICHY GOVERNMENT'S POLICE,

IN COMPLICITY WITH THE OCCUPYING NAZIS

MORE THAN 11,000 CHILDREN WERE DEPORTED FROM FRANCE

BETWEEN 1942 TO 1944,

AND WERE ASSASSINATED IN AUSCHWITZ BECAUSE THEY WERE BORN JEWISH.

MORE THAN 1000 OF THOSE CHILDREN LIVED IN THIS 20TH PARIS QUARTER.

AMONG THEM SOME ATTENDED THIS NURSERY SCHOOL.

Georges FRAJMAN 3 years old
Marie LUBELSKI 6 years old

PUPILS FROM THE ELEMENTARY SCHOOL

M-Louise Bandleider 7 years old
Regine Frajman 9 years old
Juliette Nehama 8 years old

FORMER PUPILS

Lily Frajman 15 years old
Lea gotfried 15 years old
Eva Gryncajgier 14 years old
Mina Gryncajgier 16 years old
Regine Hajman 15 years old
Chaja Hammel 17 years old
Esther Pinto 15 years old
Renee Rosenfeld 15 years old
Helene Toporeck 12 years old
Sarah Toporeck 13 years old
Madeleine Wajcman 15 years old
Lucienne Zarembovitz 16 years old
Irene Zurawski 17 years old

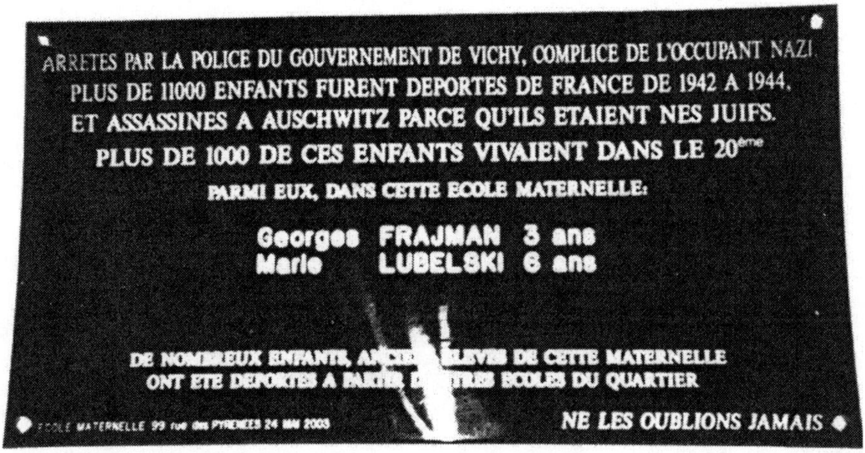
ARRETES PAR LA POLICE DU GOUVERNEMENT DE VICHY, COMPLICE DE L'OCCUPANT NAZI
PLUS DE 11000 ENFANTS FURENT DEPORTES DE FRANCE DE 1942 A 1944,
ET ASSASSINES A AUSCHWITZ PARCE QU'ILS ETAIENT NES JUIFS.
PLUS DE 1000 DE CES ENFANTS VIVAIENT DANS LE 20ème
PARMI EUX, DANS CETTE ECOLE MATERNELLE:
Georges FRAJMAN 3 ans
Marie LUBELSKI 6 ans
DE NOMBREUX ENFANTS,
ELEVES DE CETTE MATERNELLE
ONT ETE DEPORTES A
ECOLES DU QUARTIER
NE LES OUBLIONS JAMAIS

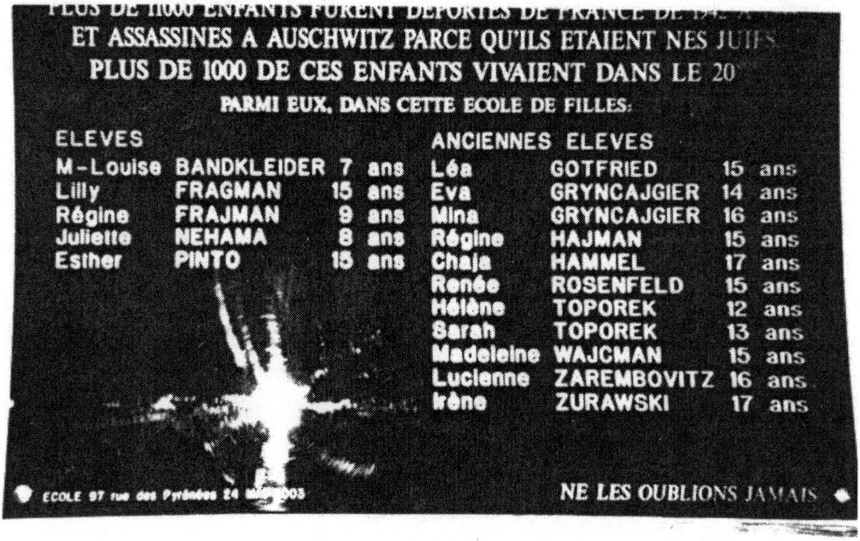
ET ASSASSINES A AUSCHWITZ PARCE QU'ILS ETAIENT NES
PLUS DE 1000 DE CES ENFANTS VIVAIENT DANS LE
PARMI EUX, DANS CETTE ECOLE DE FILLES:
ELEVES
M-Louise BANDKLEIDER 7 ans
Lilly FRAGMAN 15 ans
Régine FRAJMAN 9 ans
Juliette NEHAMA 8 ans
Esther PINTO 15 ans
ANCIENNES ELEVES
Léa GOTFRIED 15 ans
Eva GRYNCAJGIER 14 ans
Mina GRYNCAJGIER 16 ans
Régine HAJMAN 15 ans
Chaja HAMMEL 17 ans
Renée ROSENFELD 15 ans
Hélène TOPOREK 12 ans
Sarah TOPOREK 13 ans
Madeleine WAJCMAN 15 ans
Lucienne ZAREMBOVITZ 16 ans
Irène ZURAWSKI 17 ans
NE LES OUBLIONS JAMAIS

Bibliography

Adler, Jacques. *The Jews of Paris and the Final Solution.* N.Y. University, 1987.

Baruch, Olivier. *Servir l'Etat Francais.* Librairie Artheme Fayard, 1997.

Calef, Noel. *Drancy-La Faim (Drancy-Hunger)* N. Calef & FFDJF-Paris, 1991.

Conan, Eric. *Sans Oublier Les Enfants (Let us not forget the children).* Editions Grasset & Fasquelle-Paris 1991.

Davidowicz, Lucy. *The War Against the Jews 1933-1945.* New York, 1975- Havard U. press, Cambridge Massachusetts & London England 1981.

Delcampe, Paul. *Ne te Retourne Pas (Do Not Look Back)* L'Harmattan-Paris, 2001.

Delpard, Raphael. *Les Enfants Caches (Hidden Children).* Editions Jean-Claude Lattes, Paris1993.

Grynberg, Anne. Les Camps de la Honte – *Les Internes Juifs des Camps Francais. (Camps of Shame – Jewish Inmates in French Camps.)* Editions de la Decouverte-Paris 1991.

Hilberg, Paul. *The Destruction of the European Jews. 3 vol.* Holmes & Meier, New York 1985.
Klarsfeld, Serge. *Le Memorial de la Deportation des Juifs de France 1942-1944* Beate Klarsfeld Foundation-New York 1983.

Laloum, Jean. *Les Juifs de la Banlieue Parisienne* .(Jews of the Parisian Suburb) CNRS Editions – Paris 1998.
Levy, Claude & Tillard, Paul. *La Grand Raffle du Vel d'Hiv.* Robert Laffond, Paris 1967 & 1992.

Levy, Primo. *Survival in Auschwitz: The Nazi Assault on Humanity.* Summit books, New York 1986.

Marrus, Michael R.,and Paxton, Robert. *Vichy France and the Jews.* Schocken Books, New York 1983.

Poliakov, Leon. *Le Breviaire de la haine (The Breviary of Hate).* Calman- Levy, Paris 1951.

Rogerie, Andre. *Deportee 1943-1945. Temoin des Crimes Nazi Contre l'Humanite (Witness of Nazi Crimes Against Humanity)* BT Histoire Ecole Moderne Francaise, France 1992-1994.

Rosenfeld, Etienne. *De Drancy a ces Camps Dont on ne Parle Pas (From Drancy to Camps That are not Talked About)* Editions l'Hamartant, Paris 1991.

Spiegelman, Art. *Maus I & II.* Pantheon books. New York 1986-1991.

Steinberg, Paul. *Chroniques d'Ailleurs* Robert Laffont,1993.

Suhl, Yuri, ed. - *They Fought Back.* Schocken, 1967 & 1975.

Editions Talliandier. *Lettres de Drancy.(Letters from Drancy)* – Paris 2002.
Wellers, Georges. *De Drancy a Auschwitz.* CDJC. Paris 1946.

Wiesel, Eli. *Night.* Bantam Books. New York, 1960.

Zeitoun, Sabine. *Ces Enfants qu'il Fallait Sauver (The Children that Had to be Saved).* Editions Albine Michel S.A., Paris 1989.
C.D.J.C. REVUE D'HISTOIRE DE LA SHOAH
(Historical reviews of the Holocaust): Articles and Essays.
L'Activite des Organizations Juives en France sous l'Occupation (the Activities of Jewish Organizations during the German Occupation in France), Paris 1947 & 1983.

Le Statut Des Juifs – Paris, 1991 (Anti-Jewish Laws).

#120 *Du Z.A.L. au K.L., Blechhammer*– Paris,1985.

#128 *Alois Brunner et les Juifs de France*- Paris, 1987.

#141 *Il y a 50 Ans: Le Statut des Juifs* (50 Years ago the Anti-Jewish Laws by the French State). Paris, 1991.

#152 *France 1940-1945: Des Juifs de la Resistance* (Jews in the Resistance)- Paris, 1994

#153 *Le Temps des "Indesirables"* (T'was the Time of the "Indesirables"),1995.

#155 *Surtout les Enfants* (Above All, the Children)- Paris, 1995.

#161 Les Eclaireurs des Israelites de France (The French Scouts)- Paris 1997

#171 *Des Voix Sous la Cendre* (Voices from Under the Ashes)- Paris, 2001.

#175 *Le Travail du Mal* (The Labor of Crime)- Paris, 2002

Paris' Dirty Secret (Nazi Slave Labor Camps in Paris). The Jerusalem Post-Nov. 1, 2004.

Acknowledgements

I am indebted to those who helped and joined me to retrieve part of my memory world, that of a hidden child Holocaust survivor. My appreciation goes to those who shared with me their loving remembrance of deported family members, as well as their own Holocaust experience. With special thanks to Heddy Plaut Delcampe and her devoted husband Paul Delcampe; Marcel Gleiser, brother of little Annette Gleiser and son of Mr. and Mrs. Gleiser; Nicole Fain and Danielle Boruchowitz along with their friends from the Maison du Renouveau; Marcelle and her son Jojo Cogan and his son Alexandre.

I am grateful for the support and help of the staff at the CDJC *(Centre de Documentation Juive Contemporaine)* in Paris; above all to Mme Sarah Mimoun, Mr. Vidar Jacobson, and Madame Sara Halperyn. Also my acknowledgments to the staff at Yivo (Institute for Jewish Research) in New York; especially to Marek Web, to Fruma Mohrer; to the expertise of Alan Halpern, and Rob Kaplan and to many thoughtful friends: Catherine Sibon, Barbara Lichtman, Dr.Kenneth Toff, Arnold and Brenda Zaslow, Ms. Isabel Alcoff, Ms.Elaine Culbertson, Elizabeth Greenwood.

I am mostly grateful to my husband, Milton, and to Naomi, Ruth, Danielle, Jacob and Suzanne. There could be a long list of those who knowingly or unknowingly contributed and enabled me to achieve *Sarah Dreams of Pitchipoi.*

Suzanne Gross